CAN I GET A WITNESS?

HOW TO UNDERSTAND AND SET FREE A JEHOVAH'S WITNESSES

BY

BRIAN GARCIA

Cover image by Nathan Oldham

Bible Translations and abbreviations

New World Translation of the Holy Scriptures 1984- "NWT"

New International Version 2011- "NIV"

New American Standard Bible- "NASB"

American Standard Bible 1901- "ASV"

Authorized King James Version- "KJV"

New King James Version- "NKJV"

Holman Christian Standard Bible- "HCSB"

ISBN: 1492943681
ISBN 13: 9781492943686

Library of Congress Control Number: 2013919232
CreateSpace Independent Publishing Platform,
North Charleston, SC

This book is dedicated to my beautiful wife, Tatiana,
and our wonderful son, Nehemiah.
And to Jesus my Lord and my Savior;
thank you my King for saving a wretch like me.

CONTENTS

Preface   vii

Chapter 1 - Who are Jehovah's Witnesses?   1

Chapter 2 - Beliefs of Jehovah's Witnesses   9

Chapter 3 - Understanding a Jehovah's Witness   13

Chapter 4 - What's in the Name?   21

Chapter 5 - Is the Watchtower a cult?   28

Chapter 6 - God's organization or false prophets?   33

Chapter 7 - Giving a witness to Jehovah's Witnesses   43

Chapter 8 - The Jesus of the Watchtower   52

Chapter 9 - Unraveling Jesus Christ   61

Chapter 10 - Jesus according to the Scriptures   68

Chapter 11 - Making sense of the Trinity   81

Chapter 12 - Death, Heaven and Paradise   94

Chapter 13 - Is Hell not so hot?   103

Chapter 14 - The Physical Resurrection & Return of Christ   113

Chapter 15 - The Gospel Difference   123

Chapter 16 - Born Again   130

Chapter 17 - My Witness   139

PREFACE

Jehovah's Witness- The very words evoke a variety of different thoughts and opinions. Some may think of nicely groomed people knocking on people's doors on Saturday mornings, or those people who don't take blood transfusions. Others may associate Jehovah's Witnesses as a cult or a dangerous religious sect. Yet when asking the very people who bear the name, it is simply, "the truth". Depending on who you ask, you will likely get a number of comments and emotions. But who really are Jehovah's Witnesses?

This book is written by one who was born and raised in the Jehovah's Witness religion, one who loved it and learned to defend it. It is my desire to present a candid representation of the religion of my family and friends, and how the Truth of Jesus can set them free. So often when I would go door to door knocking from house to house, I often wondered where all the so-called "Christians" were. In all my days of taking the Jehovah Witness Kingdom message to the streets, I rarely ever met anyone at the door who identified themselves as a Christian and cared to share the Gospel of Jesus with me or my friends and family. My question then and now is *Can I get a witness?*

To a Christian this question is of utmost importance. Many pastors and churches in the United States and around the World are often time clueless and quite frankly stumped when asked about who the Jehovah's Witnesses are and what they believe. In fact, the answers given by many members of the church may be as vague as the opinions on top. Many times the subject of Jehovah's Witnesses is overlooked by the church, maybe even ignored or suppressed. But why has this become so? Why are born again Christians ignoring the ministry that comes straight to our door? It may be fear or a lack of understanding on what they believe. Many feel that the Jehovah Witnesses are too well versed or knowledgeable to contend with, a lot of Christians may just feel out-gunned. Unfortunately many Christians are "out-gunned" when facing a Jehovah's Witness and this must change. It has been said that a Witness can make a theological pretzel out of a regular Christian, and make even the most hardcore believer in Christ doubt what they have been taught. We have ignored a zealous and sincere group of people who have and are becoming an increasingly dangerous threat to mission fields around the globe, and the integrity of the Christian Gospel everywhere.

The purpose of this book is to inform and equip the Christian on how to better understand the zealous Witness at your door, and contend for the faith that has been delivered to the saints, and to reach the Jehovah's Witness with the true biblical message of the Gospel of Jesus Christ. (1 Peter 3:15) Before Jesus ascended into Heaven, he told his disciples, "But you will receive power when the Holy Spirit has come on you, and you will be my *witnesses* in Jerusalem, in all Judea and Samaria, and to the ends of the earth."(Acts 1:8) As Christians we cannot dismiss Jehovah's Witnesses anymore, instead with the power of the Holy Spirit we ought be witnesses of Jesus as he is "sending you to them to open their eyes and turn them from darkness to light, and from the power of Satan to God, so that they may receive forgiveness of sins and a place among those who are sanctified by faith in me."-Acts 26:17-18 NIV

CHAPTER 1

WHO ARE JEHOVAH'S WITNESSES?

Who are Jehovah's Witnesses? Many Christians believe that they are a part of a cult; others feel that they are dangerous or radical. I however will not begin this discussion with those common responses as to who the Witnesses are. I also will not resort in defaming or slamming the Jehovah's Witnesses as a "Cult" or accuse them of brain washing. No, instead I have decided to tell you a side that is seldom heard, a personal side. Why? Because to me the Jehovah's Witnesses aren't just a religious organization or a devoted group of people; no to me Jehovah's Witnesses are something far more valuable.

You see, I was born and raised in a 2nd generation Jehovah Witness home, where I learned about the Bible and applied it in my life. On weekends I'd wake up early to go to field service in the house to house ministry and when as a child in school I could not participate in Halloween or Christmas activities instead sat in the corner of the room and spoke to Jehovah. Being raised in the Jehovah Witness religion I was not given an option, I was to loyally obey and serve at all cost, and even from an early age I knew. So very zealous was I for my religion that I dedicated myself in water baptism to

Jehovah God at the age of 13, convinced it was "the truth", and I quickly began memorizing Bible verses and doctrines that could quickly refute any other point of view that I would come across. It was not long until I began interacting with Christians and with such notions as the Trinity, Hell, and the immortality of the soul. As a Witness I began refuting such Christian views and dismissed them as pagan or "demonic" in origin. I began defending the Jehovah Witness view against others at the door and even the internet; I became a Witness apologist of sorts. (The Watchtower does not endorse members debating or chatting on Jehovah's Witnesses on the internet)

Even though I am no longer a Witness today, but am now a born again follower of Christ, I don't feel the need to bash the Witnesses or speak abusively about them. Why? It is because the Witnesses are my father, my mother, my brother and my sister; my family and my friends. This isn't just some "cult" am talking about; this is the people I love and pray for. These are people who sincerely believe they have the truth and work endlessly to share it. But ultimately, these are people who are in need of the *real* truth of Jesus and his all-sufficient grace. I often think of my mother who is devoutly involved in the Witnesses till this day, I often pray and ask the Lord that while she is preaching her message from house to house, that a Christian would open their doors to her and invite her in and share the true Jesus with her. I pray that God would send her a *witness*. I am fortunate enough to still have a fair amount of contact with my immediate Witness family members, I know many ex-Jehovah's Witnesses whose parents won't even look at them. At a personal level this is why Jehovah's Witnesses matter to me, because of two generations of Witnesses I stand alone in my faith in Jesus Christ, and I long for the day that that is no longer so.

They should also matter greatly to you because the Witnesses are your neighbors, co-workers, friends, and maybe even family member. Did you know that 1 in every 261 people in the United States is one of Jehovah's Witnesses? They are all around us. If you are a Christian who takes seriously the Great Commission of our Lord Jesus to go and make disciples, then you should care greatly because the Jehovah's Witnesses are just as in need of the Gospel as is the random person you encounter on the street. If we love these people as Christ commands us to love and reach the lost, we need to vigorously do all we can to show them Christ in words and in deeds.

What I wish to present to you is a door, an open door to understand the mind and beliefs of Jehovah's Witnesses from the perspective of one who was born and raised as one. I went from vigorously defending it, to accepting

Jesus as Lord and God. It is my hope and prayer that you would take what you learn here and lead a Jehovah's Witness to freedom. If you are a person interested in contending for the faith with a Jehovah's Witness, please remember that you are dealing with a person who was been heavily indoctrinated, possibly for years on Watchtower teachings, be patient. Display the fruits of the Spirit always, and give in words and in action a witness to Jehovah's Witnesses.

In order that you may begin to better understand Jehovah's Witnesses, I will briefly highlight some of the History of Jehovah's Witnesses, to their modern day Organization and beliefs. This is not meant to be an exhaustive expository on the history of the Watchtower, many fine works are already in circulation on that hefty subject, but this is meant to merely serve as an outline to what made this religion the force it is today.

THE HISTORY OF JEHOVAH'S WITNESSES

To understand any people, one must fairly evaluate the history of that people; and thus we begin with the unique history of modern-day Jehovah's Witnesses, which began modestly enough in the late 19th century, with a young man by the name of Charles Taze Russell. Russell grew up in rural Pennsylvania, raised by tradition in the Presbyterian Church. Early on in his life he lost his mother and many of his siblings in death, which would later fuel his contempt for the Christian Church and its teachings on Hell and the afterlife, and would set the foundation for a new religion. Russell left his faith for a time and went into the Clothing business with his father, until one day he heard the preaching of a 2nd Day Adventist, Jonas Wendell. This encounter rekindled Russell's desire to formulate his own teachings, borrowing and editing existing doctrines from the Adventist movements. Russell then began associating with like-minded men and started his own "Bible Study" in 1870. Russell sold off his successful clothing business chain and began his religious venture. It was during this time that the early Bible Students(as Jehovah Witnesses were then called) really began formulating their core beliefs including rejections of Christian doctrines such as the Trinity, Hell, the immortality of the soul and many other teachings. Among the distinctive doctrines that arose during this early time in Jehovah Witness history was their belief that Jesus would return invisibly and bring a swift end to this wicked world. They began publishing their views in various religious publications, but in 1879 Russell began publishing *"Zion's Watch Tower and Herald of Christ's Presence"*, with the first issue having only 6,000 copies printed. Russell was known for brazenly attacking and debating the Christian clergymen on the theological perspectives that made the Watchtower distinct.

The group he founded was known as simply as the 'Bible Students' and it was during this time that the Bible Students began looking to the year 1914 as a very important date. For the Bible Students, Jesus Christ has already begun reigning as King being enthroned in the year 1874 and looked forward to 1914 as the year where the Bible Students would receive their heavenly reward. Concerning 1874, the Bible Students believed "Our Lord, the appointed King, **is now present, since October 1874, A. D.** according to the testimony of the prophets, to those who have ears to hear it."(The Battle of Armageddon, 1912, emphasis mine) Russell wrote in the January 15, 1892 *Zion's Watchtower* "The date of the **close** of that 'battle' is **definitely marked in Scripture as October, 1914.** It is already in progress, its beginning dating from October, 1874."(Emphasis mine) This is a very different view then that of modern day Jehovah's Witnesses; today they believe that 1914, not 1874 is the date in which Christ returned invisibly to reign and that 1914 is the beginning of the end, not the end itself. As history shows, 1914 came and went and the World did not end. Faithful Bible Students were not raptured, and Christ rule over the nations did not materialize. Many followers of Russell became disenchanted, but by large the majority of the Bible Students remained under Pastor Russell's teaching, owing a sense of loyalty to the man they believed was the "faithful and wise servant" being guided by God to reveal "meet in due season". (Matthew 24:45 KJV) A little after 1914 the end came, but it came for Charles T Russell the founder of the Watchtower Bible and Tract Society. On October 31, 1916 at the age of 64, Charles Taze Russell passed away. His followers mourned and many wondered what would become of the movement that he began.

Personally, the ministry of Charles Russell had a mystifying effect on me growing up in the religion he founded. I can recall an occasion when my local congregation took a trip to the Watchtower Farms facility in Wallkill, NY and at the visitors center there was a display of sorts that went over the history of the Organization. In that display there was a picture of a young Charles Russell and I remember seeing a sister Jehovah Witness turn to another sister and say, "Can you believe that none of this would have existed without this man."

I remember conversations with other Witnesses where they said that if Russell did not start his preaching work that the very rocks themselves would have begun to cry out! This left me with an incredible sense of awe and reverence for the man that Jehovah had supposedly chosen to set up his earthly Organization. As I continued learning about the past and history of my faith, I was astounded at the differences that evolved with the movement that Russell started and the religion that it would become. The enigma of Pastor Russell would only be complicated and amplified by those who took the lead of the Organization after his death.

After Russell's passing in 1916, an internal struggle began for the leadership and soul of the Bible Student movement. Ultimately a man by the name of "Judge" Joseph Franklin Rutherford took control of the movement in 1917 and became its President. Many Bible Students did not gravitate toward Rutherford's totalitarian approach to the Scriptures, although he was just as charismatic as Pastor Russell was. Judge Rutherford would introduce new dates, new doctrines which would greatly deviate from the original teachings of the beloved Pastor Russell, and eventually introduce a new name to the movement. The Judge would draw impressive crowds to hear him speak on topics such as *"Millions now Living will Never Die"*, a special campaign where he taught that 1925 would mark the resurrection of old faithful saints such as Abraham, Isaac and Jacob; and that eventually that would bring forth the destruction of the Nations and the restoration of the earth. Judge Rutherford believed in his own hype so much that he had a house built in San Diego, California which he named "Beth-Sarim" or House of Princes, where the Old Patriarchs would live in upon their resurrection. After the expectation the Bible Students had for the year 1925 failed to materialize, many Bible Students who remained loyal to the original teachings of Pastor Russell began to split away from the Watchtower Society and form their own congregations and Bible studies. Many of those splinter groups died off, but some remain even till this day.

Swift changes began taking place from 1917 to 1941; this era in Watchtower History is where we really begin to see the roots of the modern day movement we see today. During this time Rutherford began banning the Bible Students from celebrating "worldly" or "pagan" holidays such as Christmas, New Years, and even Mother's day. The Society became more totalitarian and sought to further differentiate itself from the rest of Christianity or as they began referring to it as 'Christendom'. By 1929 the Cross on which Christ died on became a Single beamed "torture stake", the Bible

Students began emphasizing the door to door ministry, the name "Jehovah" really began coming more and more into the fore-front. Ultimately and most importantly in the year 1931 the Bible Students adopted the name "Jehovah's Witnesses"(based upon Isaiah 43:10), forever distinguishing themselves from not only Christendom but from the various splinter groups that arose after Russell's death. In 1935 the Witnesses came to an understanding that God has set two destinies for Christians. One would be to reign with Christ in the Heavens as immortal spirit beings as members of the "anointed" 144,000 class, and the other was for a "Great Crowd" of Other Sheep to live forever in a Paradise earth. The Witnesses shut Heavens door, and began inviting all men and women to live forever on earth. Joseph Rutherford would forever change the movement that Charles Russell began by not only making vast doctrinal changes, but by establishing the Watchtower Society as God's "Theocratic" Organization, Jehovah God's sole channel of communication. As the Bible Students took upon them the name Jehovah's Witnesses, the message began growing and expanding into many countries and the Witnesses grew into over 113,000 by 1942. However in that very year, 1942 the controversial "Judge" Joseph Rutherford died in the House he built for Abraham, Isaac and Jacob, Beth-Sarim in San Diego, California. What would become of the Organization and the over 100,000 Jehovah's Witnesses around the World?

JEHOVAH'S WITNESSES IN MODERN DAY

If Russell started the movement, Rutherford innovated-it, and the new Administration would run with it. When Rutherford died, Nathan H. Knorr would be crowned the 3rd President of the Watchtower Bible and Tract Society, and during his tenure as the Society's President the Jehovah Witnesses would grow from just 113,000 to over 2 million by 1977. During this time of growth and expansion the Watchtower Society even translated and produced its own Bible Translation, known as the "New World Translation of the Holy Scriptures" or the NWT. The Witnesses produced their own Bible in the year 1950 with only the New Testament or as they refer to them as the 'Christian Greek Scriptures'. Eventually they would go on to release volumes of the Old Testament or what they refer to as the Hebrew Scriptures, until finally in 1961 they released all 66 Inspired books of the Bible in one volume. This is commonly the Bible that Jehovah's Witnesses will present to you at the door, as they claim it is a "superior translation". The Witnesses feel that all other Bible translations are the work of bias Trinitarians who smuggle in their assumptions and doctrines. Originally the Witnesses used a variety of different Translations for their publications and their door to door work; however it became increasingly necessary to produce a Bible that more closely reflected their beliefs and doctrines. They claim their Bible is without bias and were translated by top Hebrew and Greek Scholars, although the translators of the New World Translation have remained "anonymous".

By the 1950's the Watchtower began to centralize its authority by establishing a 'governing body' that would work with the President of the Society to direct the work of Jehovah's Witnesses worldwide. Many new doctrines came into play during this time, including the renowned ban on Blood Transfusions which began to take off in the medical world. The Watchtower in 1966 would begin to point to a new date in fulfillment of Bible prophecy, the year 1975. 1975 according to the Watchtower marked the 6,000th year of Human existence, and it was taught by those in authority within the Society that Christ would begin his 1,000 year reign and usher a Millennium Sabbath rest for mankind. The book, *Life Everlasting in the Freedom of the Sons of God* published by the Watchtower Society in 1966, it was stated:

"According to this trustworthy Bible chronology **six thousand years from man's creation will end in 1975… How appropriate it would be for Jehovah God to make of this coming seventh period of a thousand years a sabbath period** of rest and release, a great Jubilee sabbath for the proclaiming of liberty throughout the earth to all its inhabitants! This would be most timely for mankind. It would also be most fitting on God's part, for, remember, mankind has yet ahead of it what the last book of the Holy Bible speaks of as the reign of Jesus Christ over earth for a thousand years, the millennial reign of Christ. **It would not be by mere chance or accident but would be according to the loving purpose of Jehovah** God for the reign of Jesus Christ, the 'Lord of the Sabbath,' to run parallel with the seventh millennium of man's existence."(Emphasis mine)

A huge anticipation within the Witnesses grew concerning the year 1975. Although I was not yet born, 1975 would prove to have a profound effect on my future. In fact, if it were not for this speculation, I would likely not even exist to write this book. As Witnesses began ramping up efforts to "preach the Kingdom" message in the 1970's, on the island of Puerto Rico two Jehovah Witnesses knocked on my grandparent's door and behind that door was my mother. My mother would go on to study with the Witnesses, eventually bringing almost all her siblings into the organization. She was baptized in the year 1975. She would eventually meet my father who was also baptized around the same time and well, the rest is history.

From the 1970's onward the Jehovah's Witnesses relied not only on the President of the Watchtower Society as in the past, but they began to cling to the sole and supreme authority of the 'Governing Body', a group of "spirit-anointed" men, which when they come together are the "faithful and discreet slave" of Matthew 24:45. The Witnesses would suffer a slight loss in membership after expectations for 1975 did not materialize, however the Society would quickly sweep the matter under the rug, and during the 1980's and 90's the Witnesses would once again experience a huge increase in membership and global activity. And thus the modern story of Jehovah's Witnesses.

From humble beginnings in the turn of the 19th Century, to an army of over 7.5 million in 236 different countries by 2012, spending approximately 1.7 billion hours in spreading their message around the world. The Jehovah's Witnesses have become a force to be reckoned with. Jehovah's Witnesses are best known for their door to door evangelism, where they hand out free copies of "The Watchtower, Announcing Jehovah's Kingdom" and its counterpart, "Awake!" magazines. The Watchtower Society, the organization used by Jehovah's Witnesses, prints more Bible based literature then all the major printing presses of all the Christian denominations combined. In fact, their signature magazine 'The Watchtower' is the number one printed magazine in the entire World. In the past 10 years the Watchtower Society has printed more than 20,000,000,000 pieces of "Bible based literature". It is truly an impressive feat! The Witnesses are an extremely dedicated group of people who sincerely believe in spreading their message of the Kingdom of Jehovah God. The Jehovah Witnesses believe that they are the only True Christians in the world today, and must warn the masses of the looming threat of the end of the world, Armageddon. The Jehovah Witnesses meet together in worship in what's called a 'Kingdom Hall'. The Witnesses do not refer to their meeting places as a "church" but refer to their meetings as local congregations. At these unremarkable meetings the Witnesses are taught with a legion of "Bible aid" literature such as the Watchtower magazine on matters of living, morality, doctrine, and how to approach people at the door. The Witnesses are taught from infancy to share their faith and to be weary of association with those of who are not Jehovah's Witnesses.

CHAPTER 2

BELIEFS OF JEHOVAH'S WITNESSES

J ehovah's Witnesses are known for their distinct and peculiar beliefs, from rejecting Christmas, birthdays and Holidays as pagan, to not believing in the existence of Hell and rejecting blood transfusions, JW's are well known for their distinctness. This also means that Jehovah's Witnesses are often totally misunderstood by outsiders. Being raised in the religion I noticed how misinformed people were of our beliefs and practices, especially among those who claimed to be Christians. This encouraged me as a young Witness to be even more diligent in proclaiming my religions message and telling people about Jehovah and his purpose.

Since now you may have an idea of the History of Jehovah's Witnesses, it would be wise to also understand what they believe in. Instead of laying out an exhaustive examination of all of the complex doctrines and ideologies within the JW religion, I wish to lay out an overview of the major teachings of the Watchtower Society.

'WHAT JW'S BELIEVE IN A NUTSHELL...'

God: They believe in One uncreated personal being, who is God the Father. They believe God has a personal name and it is "Jehovah". Witnesses recognize only Jehovah as the "only True God". Calling God by name is essential in salvation and having a proper relationship with the Creator. They do not believe in the Trinity.

The Bible: They believe in the Bible as the inspired Word of God and claim that the Bible is their *sole* authority in all matters.

Jesus Christ: They believe in Jesus Christ, he was the first spirit creature that Jehovah God directly created and by means of him "all other things" were created. They also identify Jesus as Michael the Archangel, and that at his incarnation as a human he left his glory as Michael behind and became Jesus, who when he was on the earth, was only a man. They believe that Jesus became the Messiah at his baptism and that at the completion of his earthly ministry he died not upon a Cross, but a single pole or "torture stake" (NWT). When Jesus as a man died he ceased to exist until the 3rd day when Jehovah destroyed the earthly body of Jesus and recreated or "resurrected" him as a spirit creature. Upon his ascension into Heaven, he once again resumed his position as Michael the Archangel, and is now enthroned as King of God's Kingdom.

The Holy Spirit: They believe that the Holy Spirit is not a person, but is God's "active force" which he uses to fulfill his purposes. The Holy Spirit is not God or equal to God in any way.

God's original Purpose: They believe that God had created man for the purpose of living forever on a paradise earth, and that Adam and Eve through their disobedience brought mankind into sin and paradise was lost. Because of Adams sin humanity faces sicknesses, diseases, wars, famines and ultimately death. They believe that one day under God's Kingdom the earth will one day be a paradise again. They however do not believe that God will literally dwell with mankind in the Millennium rule.

Salvation: They believe that there are 2 distinct hopes or salvation class for Witnesses that do God's will and endure to the end; namely an earthly hope and a heavenly hope. They believe that only a limited number of 144,000 will inherit the heavenly Kingdom and rule with Christ, while a faithful "great crowd" of 'other sheep' will live forever on a paradise earth. In order to gain eternal life on paradise you must do the 'Kingdom' work and preach their message from door to door and live by strict adherence to the rules set out by God's mouthpiece and kingdom on earth, the Watchtower Organization. A combination of works and the "exercising faith" in the ransom sacrifice of Jesus results in salvation for the JW.

Armageddon: They believe that "the end" or Armageddon is just around the corner. They believe that ever since 1914 we have been living in the "last days" and that all the earthly governments and rulers are in a collision course to Armageddon, where Christ will act as God's executioner and wage war invisibly against Satan and his World system of things. They believe that God will massacre billions of people who are not Jehovah's Witnesses, and that only does devout and faithful through the "great tribulation" will survive the imminent Armageddon.

The Afterlife: They believe that man does not possess a soul, but *is a soul.* They believe that when a man dies his soul dies with him, and that all mankind goes into the grave or "Sheol/Hades" (The Hebrew and Greek word for the grave or 'hell'). They do not believe in a literal Hell, but that man is unconscious in death, in a sleep like state and will only awake if he is found worthy by Jehovah to receive a resurrection into the "New World". All the dead exist as a memory within the mind of God. They do not believe that all humanity will be resurrected and stand before God in Judgment, the resurrection is only reserved for the "righteous" and some of the "unrighteous" who will have a chance to conform their lives to God's will in the new system of things (aka. Paradise).

God's Kingdom: They believe that the year 1914 represents the beginning of the "last days" and the beginning of Christ second coming or presence. The Watchtower maintains that Jesus returned invisibly in that year and received "Kingdom power", or the right to rule over his Father's Kingdom. The first thing Jesus did as King was hurl Satan and his demons out of the heavenly realms as Michael the Archangel, thus resulting in World War I and other "signs" of Christ presence. The Witnesses believe Jesus will not come again physically in the flesh or that he will ever be seen by human eyes. Jesus will forever be separated from mankind, even as he "rules" over them. This teaching is in fact one of the corner stones of the religion and center of their "Good news" or Gospel, that God has established his Kingdom by Christ Jesus in the year 1914.

Other Religions: They believe that theirs is the only true religion and that all other religions are a part of "Babylon the Great", the World empire of false religion. The Witnesses believe that Christianity fell into a state of "apostasy" and was restored by Charles T. Russell. In order for one to be 'saved', he or she must come to Jehovah's organization for salvation and accept it as an expression of God's Theocratic rule for mankind. The Witnesses believe that in the year 1918 Jesus chose the Watchtower Society as God's mouthpiece and rejected 'Christendom'. They alone are True Christians.

Holidays: They believe that true Christians should be totally separate from worldly or pagan holidays such as Halloween, Christmas, New Years, Valentine's Day, Easter, 4th of July, etc. They also believe that Christians should not meddle in Politics, running for public office, voting, or saluting any flag. They do however respect their respective governments, pay taxes and obey laws that do not clash with their religious beliefs.

Blood Transfusions: They believe that the life of one's soul is in the blood; therefore Witnesses believe that blood is sacred and should not be tampered with. They believe that the Leviticus laws in the Old Testament forbid the eating or drinking of blood and equate blood transfusion as the kin to eating or drinking blood and would directly violate the laws set forth in the Bible. Out of their respect for blood and life, Jehovah's Witnesses refuse to take blood, even if it will cost their own lives or the life of a loved one.

I purposely highlighted these major teachings in Jehovah Witness theology to point out the tremendous difference between Biblical Christianity and the teachings of the Watchtower Society. It can be said that virtually every major tenet of Christian theology is turned upside down by the Watchtower; it is the total opposite of Historic Christianity. What is especially fascinating about the Witnesses is the absolute tenacity in which they attack Biblical doctrines and yet claim to hold fast to the authority of Scripture and propose that all of their teachings are derived from them.

It is one thing however to know what a particular group believes in; it is another thing to understand why they believe in their faith. Now that you have become familiarized with the history and beliefs of Jehovah's Witnesses, this next chapter will help you understand the mind and heart of a Witness from the eyes of one who was, so that you too can understand what drives them to believe in the Watchtower Society.

CHAPTER 3

UNDERSTANDING A JEHOVAH'S WITNESS

I grew up as one of Jehovah's Witnesses and many ask me how it was like was to be raised in that organization. I am often asked a variety of questions regarding my upbringing in the JW religion such as how was it to never celebrate my birthday or Christmas. To be perfectly honest, I always felt that I lived a pretty normal life as a child considering the circumstances. Sure there were things that were different than the average family in America, like waking up early on Saturday and Sunday for door to door preaching or not celebrating any holidays, but I grew up in a family of three with two loving parents who were strict yet normally understanding. I was a happy child; in fact I thank my parents for raising me with godly principles and a love for the Bible. I truly think I was a happier child because of it.

Growing up in the JW religion however did have its challenges. You see, we were taught as young people that we could not have friends that were not Jehovah's Witnesses. In fact my early life revolved so much around the Watchtower Society that I did not even know that any other religions even existed until I was in the 3rd grade. I always thought that one either served Jehovah or they were a "bad person". The only way I could make friends

- 13 -

in school was if I talked to them about the Bible, and so there I was, in the 3rd grade preaching to my classmates and even my teachers about Jehovah. Teachers and students were fascinated with what I had to say, although throughout my years in School I would become the center of ridicule and often time be totally alone because of my faith. I felt disconnected with other kids, even kids at the Kingdom Hall. I was taught that everything in the world was "bad" and I can remember having to watch certain cartoon programs in secret because of fear that my parents would see it and condemn it as "worldly". I was always weary of making friends outside the congregation because I knew my parents would not approve of my "worldly" associations. Even as a child there was always the expectation to be perfect or a close to perfect as you could get. In the Witness culture you are always being compared to others, especially growing up in it. I would often time feel like I was not as "spiritual" as the other kids, or that I did not do enough to make Jehovah happy. I often time felt alone and unworthy.

Being disconnected from other youths I would turn to God and ask him to be my friend. I would try and find comfort by reading the Bible or spending time with family for the majority of them are Witnesses. My life from birth revolved around the JW community, all I would come to know and love had its Genesis and Revelation in the Watchtower Society. However I refuse to see myself as a victim, or as a person who had their childhood stripped away from them. Although I was deprived of certain functions that other children and families partake in, I was still a fun loving child who grew up with an intense love and reverence for God. I am thankful for my experiences, and I am blessed to see how God's hand has been upon my life from the beginning.

WHY I BELIEVED...

If you are not one of Jehovah's Witnesses you may just being saying to yourself, "How in the world can anyone believe in some of those teachings?" If you are a Christian you may be wondering where they even find support in the Scriptures for some of their beliefs. To me this brings me into a time of reflection, a time in which I examine why I believed in this religion and why I defended it so passionately. First it is important to note this, whether you were born in the Witness religion or you were converted at the door, once you are in there is an over whelming feeling of being a part of something bigger then yourself.

The Jehovah's Witnesses boast about how 'united' they are all over the world and how they share in a worldwide brotherhood. They claim that their "unity" is a mark of them being the "True Religion". As a Witness you really do begin to feel the magnitude of these statements when going to a district convention where thousands of Witnesses meet together for a weekend and fill a stadium. Something that made me feel especially warm was when visiting other states or even my home island of Puerto Rico, seeing my fellow Witnesses walking down the Street with their "Watchtower" and "Awake!" magazines in hand preaching the message. Even when passing by a Kingdom Hall as we took our family vacations around the Country made me feel warm and smug, especially when seeing or passing by the divided churches of 'Christendom'. This type of work or unity is seldom seen or heard of in other religious circles, and this feature alone attracts many people to the Organization, this unreal serene sense of unity with people you have never even met. What I would later find out, this so-called unity was actually conditional upon you accepting the terms and conditions of the Watchtower Society. If I or another Witness began developing different views on certain doctrinal topics, our bond of "brother" or "sister" would quickly be diminished. It is a false unity based upon uniformity and conformity. True unity however, cannot be forced; it can only be experienced in the context of true love and freedom.

Nevertheless, as long as you accept their terms and agreements, the so-called unity amongst Jehovah's Witnesses is compelling. Once you accept and are then accepted into the Jehovah Witness community you begin to build your life around it, you may have to begin to let go of some friends who are not Witnesses, you may have to stop attending family holiday functions. Or if you were raised in a Witness family like I was, it quickly stops being just a religion; it becomes a way of life.

As a child I would often flip through the publications of the Watchtower and look at all the beautiful depictions of Paradise earth. I could see myself in those pictures enjoying eternal life with my family forever in a restored earth where no one would ever grow old and die. Where sickness was only a thing of the past and where even the animals dwell in harmony with mankind. It was mesmerizing.

Most Witnesses are brought to believe that there only hope is to live forever on a Paradise Earth; this teaching captivates the hearts of many. I mean who wouldn't want to live forever and never get old or get sick and die? The very quest of all mankind and its religions is to find the key to immortality and eternal peace. The Witnesses come to you with compelling answers, they have been prepared to share with you a multitude of Scriptures that talks about the meek inheriting the earth, the unrighteous being cut off, and a new world being established. One of the reasons I believe many people become Jehovah's Witnesses is because of this hope. Some people aren't looking for the most convincing answers, some people may not be looking for fame or power, and some people are just looking for hope. The notion of Paradise was hope, and while other religions taught about some vague concept of Heaven in the great beyond, a paradise earth was tangible, something I could relate too. I know that for me and many other Witnesses, Paradise was our motivation... And I couldn't wait to tell others about it!

I believed. I believed with a passion, and it was not only because of the prospect of everlasting life in a paradise, but because as a Jehovah's Witness I felt like I had answers. This is significant in order to understand Jehovah's Witnesses; they know why they believe what they believe, and they are passionate about it. The average Witnesses is very well versed in the Scriptures and know exactly what Bible verses to use for conversations at the door, when witnessing on the streets, when offering practical advice to fellow believers, and almost any situation that may come up. It would never cease to amaze me how my mother could open her Bible and defend our beliefs every time someone had a tough question at the door. I had a level of security growing up because of the way we as Jehovah's Witnesses seemingly had an answer to everything.

When I was about 12 years old I was determined to step up and begin to study and understand my faith. I began to read the Bible and Watchtower Publications on my own for pleasure, and it would be very soon that I myself began memorizing Bible verses, understanding theological topics that the majority of young Christian people at that age could not even begin to comprehend. The more I memorized and the more I knew, the more confident I felt that I truly had "the Truth". And I suppose that's what it really comes down to for the JW; they feel for the majority that they have "the truth". I can recall moments where I had brief interactions with Christian kids my age in grade school; these kids could not recount accurate Bible stories, had no memorization of Scripture, and most importantly didn't have any answers. When a religious or Biblical discussion would arise in School, the kids would go right past the Pentecostal kids, right past the Baptist kids, right past the Catholic kids and go straight to me for answers. I had answers, satisfying answers that came from the Bible. I could have taken any topic mentioned in the previous pages on the beliefs of the Watchtower and convinced the average person that the belief was rooted in the Bible. We were taught to use the Bible through the lens of the interpretations of the Watchtower.

Further evidence to me that I had the truth was the simple fact that we alone as Jehovah's Witnesses preached the "Kingdom message" or Good News from house to house. Now this is a huge deal to JW's and often time they will ask the Christian "Well if *you* have 'the Truth', then why don't you take your message from house to house like the disciples did in Jesus time?" It made sense to me. I mean Jesus sent out his disciples to go and preach the Kingdom. Jesus before ascending to Heaven told his followers to "go therefore and make disciples of people of all nations"! (Matthew 28:19) As a Jehovah's Witness, this is was a divine command to make Jehovah's name known. No matter what your opinion is of the Witnesses, they are to be admired for their work and zeal in spreading their message far and wide. The Christian Church can learn a great deal from the Witnesses and their method. It was because of this work or "sign" I could point too as a tangible evidence of my religion being the one True Christian faith.

FEAR AND ARMAGEDDON

If the promise of paradise won't do it for you, then possibly the fear of Armageddon will. Alongside the beautiful depictions of paradise earth, was the horrifying and scarring depictions of the one thing Jehovah's Witnesses fear most, Armageddon. I can recall the look of utter terror and horror on the faces of those being destroyed by God at Armageddon in the pictures depicted in the pages of Watchtower publications, including the children's books. In my mind only two options were available, serve Jehovah and live forever in a paradise earth, or disobey Jehovah and be destroyed forever.

The Watchtower Society has always capitalized on fear; this is a religion that came into existence during a time when religious fervor and anticipation for Christ Second Coming was at an all-time high. The Watchtower throughout its history has claimed that the "End" was near, even predicting Christ presence and the destruction of this system of things multiple times. I grew up being told that I would probably never see High School because the end was so near. I was told that I would probably get married in the new system since Armageddon would have already arrived by the time I would be old enough to marry. Witnesses are constantly being reminded that the End is near, and the only way to survive is through association with the Watchtower.

"In these last days of the present system of things, Jehovah's people are making known Gods righteous standards and are declaring good news about the possibility of surviving into the new world. (2 Peter 3:9-13) Just as Noah and his God-fearing family were preserved in the ark, **survival of individuals today depends on** their faith and their loyal **association with the earthly part of Jehovah's universal organization.** (*The Watchtower,* May 15, 2006)

That fear even creeps into the daily lives of every JW. I met an ex-Jehovah's Witness who was converted to the organization in his early 20's, that he was constantly in fear of Armageddon, so much so that every time he heard a thunder storm he felt as though he could be destroyed at any second. He felt as if God was going to "blow him up" at the moment he did something wrong. This is a real fear, a fear instilled in me from childhood, from as far back as I remember. The "end" was always just around the corner, even as a child my parents would motivate me to get out of bed and go to field service because "Armageddon was close" and I needed to be a good boy and be out there doing Jehovah's will... or else. Many sincere Jehovah's Witnesses are not solely involved in this group out of genuine love for Jehovah, but out of a deep rooted fear of being destroyed by the God they serve at Armageddon. I truly believed growing up that the Great Tribulation would begin before I even entered High School, I would day dream about me and my family going underground to avoid the coming persecution of the Witnesses.

ACCEPTING WATCHTOWER AUTHORITY

Every individual will always have his or her reason for believing in their faith, the seed of paradise and Armageddon implanted in my head as a child would grow and sprout into a genuine love for my Creator, and a longing to know him and share him with others. I learned that once you accepted the attracting aspects of the religion, you will eventually begin to accept the vague and even ridiculous aspects of the religion without even questioning. Why? Because you have already bought in, you are already emotionally invested. And this does not simply refer to only the Jehovah's Witnesses, but even to some Christians. Some of us as Christians just begin accepting things without putting it through the biblical test and examining the Scriptures; we may simply believe things because some Pastor or special speakers have told us to believe in something. No doubt this principle can be applied to almost anyone with a set of religious conviction. But what makes Jehovah's Witnesses unique in this sense is how far they will take their obedience.

You see, obedience is a test of loyalty, and "Jehovah's Organization" demands all of it. This is an obedience that will put your religion over members of your own family, an obedience that will ask you never to question or have an "independent mind", an obedience that will ask you to even lay down your life in refusal to have a blood transfusion. To be one of Jehovah's Witnesses, you must obey. Obey at all cost. The Watchtower has said the following regarding independent thinking:

"From the very outset of his rebellion Satan called into question God's way of doing things. **He promoted independent thinking**… How is such independent thinking manifested? A common way is **by questioning the counsel that is provided by God's visible organization**… As we study the Bible we learn that Jehovah has always guided his servants in an organized way. And just as in the first century there was only one true Christian organization, **so today Jehovah is using only one organization**. (Ephesians 4:4, 5; Matthew 24:45-47) Yet there are some who point out that the organization has had to make adjustments before, and so they argue: "This shows that we have to make up our own mind on what to believe." **This is independent thinking**. " (*The Watchtower*, Jan. 15, 1983)

Such statements almost made me afraid to think for myself; instead I would trust in what I was being told and hanged on their every word. My eternal destiny lay in their hands as I subjected my mind to their will and authority. Many Witnesses without even noticing are enslaved by an idea; the idea that their Organization alone is the sole channel of truth, the Watchtower heavily promotes this concept in their literature and brazenly states its authority and waves it in the face of its followers.

As a Witness I had no problem with this concept, I mean, why wouldn't I obey the Organization that God was using as his sole channel of communication! If the Organization asks me to do something it is because Jehovah God himself has commanded it. You are taught to be faithful and loyal to the Watchtower Society, as you would be to God and Christ. And The Watchtower has not been afraid in exhorting its power and authority over the lives of Jehovah's Witnesses. You see the Witness version of Jehovah was so tightly connected to the organization of the Watchtower, that to obey Jehovah meant we had to obey the Society. And vice versa, disobeying the organization was in effect disobeying God himself.

Jehovah Witnesses are in effect slaves to a concept, an illusion. They are taken captive by the lie that these men in the Watchtower headquarters are God's chosen instrument and that by following them they can have a right relationship with God. The Witness knows deep down in their heart as I did, that to question the "Society" is to question God himself. The Watchtower has set itself in the place of Christ in the hearts of millions of Jehovah's Witnesses. They refer to their organization as "the truth", that only by associating with God's "channel of communication" could one attain everlasting life. (*The Watchtower*, Feb. 15, 1983, p. 12)

Jesus is subtly stripped away of his place as "the Truth" incarnated and the only way to the Father. (John 14:6) The Witness will forever be in bondage to men until they acknowledge that "the Truth" is not found in a religious organization or church, but in the very Person of Jesus Christ himself.

CHAPTER 4

WHAT'S IN THE NAME?

Jehovah's Witnesses are unique in their use of the divine name of God, Jehovah. In matter of fact some people who may hear the name "Jehovah" may immediately associate the divine name with the religious organization that bears its name; Jehovah's Witnesses. Why do they emphasize the name Jehovah so much and why do most mainstream Christian denominations rarely make mention of it? What does it mean to bear the name of *Jehovah's Witness?*

Growing up in the organization gave me a sense of pride and privilege, that we alone in all the earth had the divine right to bear the name, *Jehovah's* Witnesses! I believe one of the most convincing reasons why a person could come to believe in the Jehovah Witness message could be directly linked to their usage and identification of Jehovah as the name of the one True God. How can the usage of one name be such a compelling drive to become or remain a Jehovah's Witness? There is power in the Name.

WHY SO IMPORTANT?

If you asked the average person what God's name is, you'd likely get answers like "God is his name" or "Lord". Many are shocked and surprised when one of Jehovah's Witnesses reveal to them even in their own Bibles that God does have a name, Jehovah. You see the name "Jehovah" or what is commonly referred to as the Tetragrammaton represented by the four letters YHWH in the Hebrew appears 6,828 times in the Old Testament or Hebrew Scriptures. The Witnesses correctly bring out the fact that the words "Lord" and "God" are merely titles and not proper names for the God of the Bible.

In Exodus 3:15 God says to Moses "Jehovah(YHWH: Yahweh) the God of YOUR forefathers, the God of Abraham, the God of Isaac and the God of Jacob, has sent me to YOU.' This is my name to time indefinite, and this is the memorial of me to generation after generation." (NWT) Many times when knocking on the door the Witness will invite you to read in your King James Version of the Bible Psalms 83:18 which read's "That men may know that thou, whose name alone is Jehovah, art the most high over all the earth."(The 1 of 4 times the name "Jehovah" appears in the KJV) I can remember personally a witnessing experience I had with a school mate who was brought up in the Pentecostal Church, I brought up the point that in her English Bible anytime the word "the LORD" is in capital letters, the Tetragrammaton (Which means the Four letter name of God in Hebrew) YHWH the name Yahweh or Jehovah is being substituted. Yet when she would read her Spanish version of the Bible, "La Reina Valera" the Spanish word for Jehovah is used consistently throughout the Old Testament. This perplexed her, why did most English Translations of the Bible refuse to iden- tify God by name? Why give the Almighty Author of the Bible mere titles, why hide the name?

I as one of Jehovah's Witnesses had the answers. This is a compelling aspect to the religion, they have built an extraordinary conspiracy theory that the reason why 'Christendom' (A word used by JW's to identify false Christianity) does not use the name "Jehovah" in public preaching or wor- ship and in Bible Translation is because they hate God's name and are in the control and bidding of Satan the Devil. Who doesn't like a good conspiracy theory?

To the Witness, the name 'Jehovah' is the key. So passionate they were to differentiate themselves from the rest of Christendom and to proclaim God's divine name that they took upon the name of God as the title of their religion back in the early 1930's. Growing up in the organization I could not be more proud to bear the name of my God Jehovah, it was a duty and a privilege. We were taught that there was no greater honor then to bear and keep the name Jehovah's Witnesses. We were His *witnesses*! In fact in the 2010 Year Book of Jehovah's Witnesses, published by the Watchtower Society there is a letter from the Governing Body, the "anointed" 8 men taking the lead over 7 million Witnesses wrote this concerning Jehovah's name:

"What a privileged people we are to bear the name of the Universal Sovereign, Jehovah! That name is eternal, imperishable, and incomparable. **It was Jehovah who gave us his name to bear**, and especially since the year 1931, we have been identified with that distinctive name. (Isa. 43:10) It is with unreserved pride that we identify ourselves as **Jehovah's Witnesses**.

The Devil relentlessly tries to blot out the name of God. Under his control, the nations spurn Jehovah's name. **Babylon the Great, the world empire of false religion, hates the divine name and has removed it from many Bible translations**. In contrast, Jesus held high his Father's name, giving it first place in the model prayer he taught his followers... Later, in heartfelt prayer to his Father, he said: "I have made your name manifest to the men you gave me out of the world." (John 17:6) Following Jesus' fine example, we are more determined than ever to herald Jehovah's name vigorously throughout the earth."(Emphasis mine)

Apart from knowing Jehovah's name in Watchtower Theology you cannot be saved from this system of things. In their Translation of Romans 10:13 it reads "Everyone who calls on **the name of Jehovah** will be saved." To the Witness it isn't the name of Jesus Christ that saves, it is the name Jehovah. The Watchtower has written a wealth of literature on this matter alone, it is rooted deeply in their identity.

The Watchtower Society in their zeal and devotion to the name Jehovah, have taken it upon themselves to insert the divine name 237 times into their translation of the Christian Greek Scriptures, although no Greek New Testament manuscript in existence contains the divine name therein. The Watchtower in their New World Translation of the Holy Scriptures have taken the Greek word for 'Lord' (Kurios) and at their discretion translated it as Jehovah. This is a result of their theological bias and insistence that the original writers knew, and used the name Jehovah.

JEHOVAH, LORD OR YAHWEH?

Jehovah's Witnesses are pretty adamant that the only name that true Christians should use and make known is the name, Jehovah. Is the name "Jehovah" an accurate translation of the Hebrew Tetragrammaton? Well the name "Jehovah" is a late 11th century, Latin inspired pronunciation of the Tetragrammaton with the combined vowels of the Hebrew word Adonai ("Lord" in Hebrew). The Hebrew Tetragrammaton, transliterated as YHWH, was written only in consonants and because of superstitious views the Jews ceased pronouncing the Name, substituting it for the Hebrew Adonai. So in reality, no one really knows how the divine name, YHWH, is pronounced. Nevertheless, in the 11th century Catholic monks decided to combine the vowels of Adonai and add them to the Latinized version of YHWH (IHVH), where they came up with Iehovah, and ultimately with Jehovah in later English renderings. The rendering "Jehovah" is by no means the correct pronunciation of the Tetragrammaton, but it was a good attempt to translate the forgotten most sacred name of God. Today, it is almost universally accepted by Hebraic Bible scholars that the most correct pronunciation for the Tetragrammaton is Yahweh. Even the Watchtower Society has admitted in its writings that the name ""Yahweh" is favored by most Hebrew scholars", while also acknowledging that many Biblical names "can all be derived from Yahweh". (*Insight*, published by WTS)

Why then do Jehovah's Witnesses continue to be so adamant and pushy toward using the pronunciation "Jehovah" instead of the more correct form *Yahweh*? The Watchtower Society answers, "Many scholars favor the spelling "Yahweh," but it is uncertain and there is not agreement among them. On the other hand, "Jehovah" is the form of the name that is most readily recognized, because it has been used in English for centuries". (*Reasoning from the Scriptures*) The Society argues that the spelling "Jehovah" is more recognized and used throughout English history, thus in keeping with that tradition they feel like there is no reason to sacrifice the more "readily recognized" name Jehovah, in favor of the more accurate and pure name, Yahweh. It is interesting to note that JW's despise the Christian tradition in using the word "Lord" in place of Jehovah, yet they also appeal to a non-biblical tradition is favoring Jehovah over Yahweh.

This also brings up a great question for self-examination, if modern Bible scholars and even the Watchtower Society agree that the name *Yahweh* is an accurate rendition of the Tetragrammaton, then why do most Christian Bibles translate the Name as "the LORD" throughout the Old Testament?

As noted before, around 200 years before Christ, the Jews out of fear and reverence for the divine name, stopped pronouncing it out loud, and instead substituted the name for Adonai which is "Lord" in Hebrew. It seems like throughout Church history and into modern times, the Church has maintained a superstitious tradition that originated with the Jews and has no bases for in the Scriptures. The word 'Lord' is not even an attempt to translate the Tetragrammaton, and in this respect, I must give the JW's credit, they at least attempt to use a translation of the divine name. Where the Witnesses I feel go wrong is that they insist that God will somehow not listen or honor the prayers of people who do not use the name and pronunciation, Jehovah. They believe that *their* rendering and interpretation of the Name is the correct one, and thus the one God himself approves. While I believe that it is the principle of the Name that God wants us to hold high as sacred, regardless if you use Yahweh or Jehovah. In Isaiah 12:4 we read, "Give thanks to Yahweh; **proclaim His name**! Celebrate His works among the peoples. Declare that **His name is exalted**." (HCSB) In order to proclaim his Name we must first know it and use it! To exalt and declare God's name also means that we must love it, and I do believe that ignoring God's personally revealed name which appears more than any other name in Scripture and substitute it for a title is a dishonoring of the God of the Bible. I also believe that the Witnesses also make God's name in vain by the extreme usage of it. The name Jehovah is in almost every sentence in their literature and during their public talks in the Kingdom Hall. They use the name Jehovah so much that I believe it has taken away the value and holiness and reverence that the Scriptures tell us to have. There is such repetition of the name that it becomes mundane devoid of all meaning.

Nevertheless, using the title "LORD" in place of Yahweh gives the Witnesses a foothold, many JW's that I personally knew and grew up around left their churches and converted to the Watchtower because it was the Witnesses who pointed out to them that God has a personal name, something that the many of the Churches failed to teach them. I do not object however to using the title "LORD" or reading from Bibles that have them instead of Yahweh, for God is certainly Lord and is a title that reveals God's power and attributes. Jesus in fact uses the title Lord for himself and for God many times throughout the New Testament, and even refers to God as "Father" and tells us to address him as "Father" instead of "Jehovah". (Matthew 6:9) So since Jesus didn't teach us to use the Tetragrammaton, does that mean we shouldn't use it? No, for in light of the fact that Jesus is himself the highest revelation of God, the very name of Jesus means "Yahweh is our Salvation", so in Jesus we meet the very God who we are commanded to proclaim and make known.

DOES GOD'S NAME REALLY MATTER?

Should the name of God actually be important to Christians today, if so should we use "Jehovah" or "Yahweh" as the proper name? This is an area I must painfully agree with the Jehovah's Witnesses in, God's name does matter! For centuries the Church has followed in the traditions of men in suppressing the divine name of God. Today I prefer to use the more proper and accurate name Yahweh, although I have little objection to the use of the name Jehovah. I feel like Christians have forgotten a precious gem of our History and faith. The sad reality is, the Jehovah's Witnesses make a tremendous point and the Church needs to stop making dead centuries old theological arguments against the name of our God and "Seek Yahweh and live"!(Amos 5:6 HCSB) Indeed, "**The name of Yahweh** is a strong tower; the righteous run to it and are protected."(Proverbs 18:10) I am thrilled to see many English Translations of the Bible begin to restore the Covenant name of God back into the Bible. One thing I want to make perfectly clear is that the Name of God does not belong to the Jehovah's Witness; it does not originate with the Witnesses. I have a deep appreciation for the knowledge of growing up calling God by name. As a Christian today I am adamantly interested in seeing the name of God restored to the Bride of Jesus Christ. In fact, it is still woven into the very fabric of who I am. The Name properly belongs to the children of God redeemed by Yahweh and we must reclaim it! God's name matters because it matters to Him. Remember, this is how God as revealed himself to us in Scripture, "**Yahweh**, the God of your fathers, the God of Abraham, the God of Isaac, and the God of Jacob, has sent me to you. This is **My name forever**; this is how I am to be **remembered in every generation**." (Exodus 3:15, HCSB)

I suppose you can say that it is because of my background in this matter that I take seriously the charge to know and love God's name. While there is no doubt that because of my upbringing this is a topic serious and dear to my heart, and I truly believe that as we begin to reclaim God's proper name in our lives and worship, the Witnesses will have less of a stronghold on the name of our God. But where I failed in as a Jehovah's Witness was that I only knew God by name, but in reality I had no idea of who he really was as a person. How was that so? That is because one can only know Jehovah in the Person and Work of our Lord Jesus Christ. Where the Witnesses fall dangerously short is in their view of who Jesus Christ is, and there is no greater topic for the Jehovah Witness and the Christian to engage in then who Christ is.

CHAPTER 5

IS THE WATCHTOWER
A CULT?

How do we define a Cult? In our modern day culture, the word "Cult" has become a dirty word, having the connotations of being "secretive, unorthodox or dangerous". The word is thrown around a lot and has a very subjective nature to it, but is the religion of Jehovah's Witnesses "secretive, unorthodox and dangerous"? Admittedly this is a topic that I have avoided throughout this book until now. Why? Because my intention with this book has been to give you, the reader, a perspective that is different from what has been written and published by critics and opponents of the Watchtower Society. I am a product of a loving Jehovah Witness family, although I am no longer a Jehovah's Witness and clearly have differing views on Jesus and the Bible; I yet feel no need to label the ones I love and want to reach out to, a dangerous cult.

On the other side, because of my convictions as a Christian, and because of my experiences I know that there are legitimate reasons to view the Organization that dictates to Jehovah's Witnesses worldwide as secretive, unorthodox and certainly as dangerous. I want to be careful here, it is so easy to start labeling and attacking a faith because we disagree with it, and that is not what I or any other Christian should be about. But we also need to heed the Scriptural counsel to "Have nothing to do with the fruitless deeds of darkness, but rather expose them". (Ephesians 5:11 NIV) If the Watchtower Society is truly leading Jehovah's Witnesses down a road of darkness, it is our responsibility as Christians who share in the light of Jesus to expose the deeds of darkness, so that the Jehovah Witness can witness the light of the Gospel of Jesus. (2 Corinthians 4:4-6) So as regards to this topic, it is our duty to examine the deeds of those in leadership of the Watchtower and hold them accountable to the Word of God.

HOW DO JEHOVAH'S WITNESS VIEW THEMSELVES?

This is an important question because it deals with how the average Witness has been taught to view themselves as part of this worldwide movement, and how in effect to view everyone else outside of the walls of their organization. So how do the Witnesses view their religion?

To the Jehovah's Witness, their religion and organization is "the truth", the only true religion. The book *"Reasoning from the Scriptures"* states "Because Jehovah's Witnesses base all of their beliefs, standards of conduct, and organizational procedures on the Bible, their faith in the Bible itself as God's Word gives them the conviction **that what they have is indeed the truth**". Not only do they believe that they have the truth, but they believe that only their organization can properly interpret sacred Scripture.

"**Only this organization functions for Jehovah's purpose and to his praise**. To it alone God's Sacred Word, the Bible, is not a sealed book," (*Watchtower,* July 1, 1973)

Jehovah's Witnesses believe that they exclusively have God's truth, God's blessing and God's leading. So can individuals ever come to an accurate knowledge of God by just reading the Bible? According to the Watchtower, the answer is no. "All who want to understand the Bible should appreciate that the "greatly diversified wisdom of God" **can become known only through Jehovah's channel of communication**, the faithful and discreet slave". (*The Watchtower*, Oct. 1, 1994)

The Witness believes that they are "in the truth" in so long as they are "in the organization", God's only channel of communication. The Watchtower clearly teaches that the rest of the World, especially professing Christians in "Christendom" are in complete spiritual darkness, and that only by coming to them as God's sole channel, can any man ever come to know the truth of God's Word. In essence they deny the sufficiency of the Bible and the Holy Spirit to lead man to God, and set themselves as the middle men, the mediators between God and man. So in a way, it's not so much how does the average JW view themselves, but it's really how they view their organization. The organization claims to have *hidden* or *secret* knowledge about the Bible that has been directly revealed to them, and kept hidden from the religions of the world.

They view everyone outside of the organization as "worldly" and under the influence of Satan the Devil. The Watchtower instills paranoia and even a fear of everything outside its walls. Growing up a Witness, I wasn't allowed to have worldly friends or go to parties or parks where there were no Witness children in. Psychologically as a child growing up in that type of exclusive religious mentality, I was raised with an "us vs. them" mindset. I looked down upon my non-Witness schoolmates and felt a sense of superiority over them because I would be spared in Armageddon and they likely wouldn't. Living under the influence of the Watchtower left such a mark on me as a young person, I felt as if I had a special knowledge that the world didn't have, that my schoolmates and even my teachers didn't have. I had "the truth", while everyone else lived the lie. To be fair however, Witnesses are encouraged to go out and preach their controversial message to their neighbors and friends, but it won't be until many months of studying with them that they begin to unfold the importance of the authority and exclusivity of the organization and its "faithful and discreet slave". But as soon as someone within the walls of the Watchtower begins to question or think independently from the organization, they are quickly disfellowshipped, cut off from the congregation, loved ones, friends and family. There is no room for independence or critical thinking within the organization. As noted in previous chapters, the organization has published articles discouraging its members from thinking independently.

So because of the exclusive nature of the Watchtower Society, I believe it is certainly fair when evaluating the evidence, to say that the Watchtower definitely meets the criteria of being "secretive" and exclusive.

But are they unorthodox and dangerous?

To be secretive is one thing, but to be unorthodox and even dangerous are much more serious charges. Unless you've been reading a totally different book this entire time, it is clear that the beliefs and practices of Jehovah's Witnesses are definitely unorthodox by virtue of breaking away from Historic and Biblical Christianity. For example the Witnesses deny the deity of our Lord Jesus Christ, claiming he is Michael the Archangel, and that he died on a torture stake instead of a cross. They also deny Christ physical resurrection from the dead; they deny the Biblical teaching on the afterlife, and many more essential Christian teachings. As a Born again Christian, I believe the Jehovah's Witnesses misrepresent the Scriptures, not only that but they just miss the whole picture. While the JW focuses on being in an organization, the Bible tells us to test ourselves to see if we are in the faith by being in Christ Jesus! (2 Corinthians 13:5) Jesus is the litmus test, not what organization or denomination we belong too. The Bible makes clear that one is either in Christ or he is not, one is either saved or lost, spiritually alive through new birth, or spiritually dead in the flesh. According to the testimony of Scripture, the beliefs and doctrines of Jehovah Witnesses are contrary to sound teaching as we have received them in the New Testament. (Titus 3:1) This in effect makes the organization of Jehovah's Witnesses very dangerous, as it sets itself in the place of Christ and denies its adherents the gift of eternal life. The stinging word of Jesus to the Pharisees is fitting in regard to the leadership of Jehovah's Witnesses:

"Woe to YOU, scribes and Pharisees, hypocrites! **because YOU shut up the kingdom of the heavens before men; for YOU yourselves do not go in, neither do YOU permit those on their way in to go in**". (Matthew 23:13, NWT)

Spiritually speaking, the Watchtower Society is unorthodox and incorrect in their teachings, and are very dangerous in the sense that they are leading people to men instead of leading them to Christ. There are many other legitimate reasons why many consider the Watchtower are a dangerous cult, such as how they separate families through their disfellowshipping policies, or how they endanger lives because of their no blood transfusion policies. These are legitimate concerns that the Watchtower Society has yet to rectify, and manmade teachings that are destructive which the men leading the Society will have to give an account to God Almighty for. The Watchtower Society most definitely meets the criteria of a cult, from their obsessive reverence of their organization and its "faithful slave class", to their fear or hatred of all things outside their faith, and most importantly their denial of the Person and work of Jesus Christ.

But let this reality come with a warning, yes they do meet the criteria of being a cultic religion which suppresses and oppresses people and ideas contrary to their dogma, but we need to look ourselves in the mirror and watch ourselves lest we become just like them. You see I grew up "name calling" people who were not Jehovah's Witnesses. If you were not one of Jehovah's Witnesses you were worldly, apostate, liar, false teacher, false Christian, pagans, hypocrite, satanic. I had a word for everyone who was not a Witness. Name calling creates a wall, the person doing the name calling or the labeling feels as if he or she has a sense of authority over the person or group being labeled. And the people being labeled have a sense of persecution because of the name calling, thus justifying their worldview. It's a He said She said type of affair, and True Christians should have nothing to do with that. Our primary concern should be the souls of the Jehovah's Witness we are reaching out to, and this applies to any particular group we may be ministering to. If we get wrapped in labeling and name calling we become no better than the Witness who has been labeling us.

Yes, the individual Witnesses are involved in a very dangerous religious organization, but instead of creating more walls, start praying and working towards leading them to the one who breaks down the dividing walls of hostility, our Lord Jesus Christ. (Ephesians 2:14)

CHAPTER 6

GOD'S ORGANIZATION OR FALSE PROPHETS?

The concept that God has used and is directing an earthly organization to communicate and advance his purposes is central to the structure and theology of Jehovah's Witnesses. The Jehovah's Witnesses believe that God has been using the Watchtower Bible and Tract Society as an earthly representation of God's heavenly kingdom. The Witnesses believe that only their organization is guided by God's Holy Spirit, and that "Unless we are in touch with this **channel of communication** that God is using, we will not progress along the road to life, **no matter how much Bible reading we do**." (*The Watchtower*, Dec. 1, 1981)

The Watchtower Society has taken upon itself the title of the "faithful and discreet slave" from their translation of Matthew 24:45, they believe that they are God's appointed channel to feed God's people, "food at the proper time". Throughout Watchtower history the specific interpretation and identity of the "faithful slave" has changed many times, even in recent times. During the infancy of the Society's history, it was believed that Charles T Russell was God's appointed channel or the "faithful and wise servant". *The Watchtower* of December 1st, 1919 stated this regarding Russell: "Thousands of the readers of Pastor Russell's writings believe that **he filled the office** of "**that faithful and wise servant,**" and that his great work was giving to the Household of Faith meat in due season. His modesty and humility precluded him from openly claiming this title, but he admitted as much in private conversation". That view was adjusted in the late 1920's when the Watchtower began to teach that it applied to all "spirit anointed Christians" who made up the remnant of the 144,000. In the 1950's the Watchtower began appointing a "governing body" made up of 'anointed Christians' which would be the mouthpiece of the "slave class" and focus on matters of organizational policy and doctrine.

In even more recent times, the Watchtower Society has made a tremendous change in their view of who is the "faithful and discreet slave". In October of 2012 at the Watchtowers annual meeting, members of the Governing Body announced "new light" (a term used by JW's when a new interpretation of Scripture is taught), that the Governing Body of Jehovah's Witnesses is the "faithful and discreet slave" and that the remnant of the 144,000 should no longer be considered a part of the "slave class", but that they are now a part of the "belongings" of Christ appointed slave, the 8 men on Governing Body. The "new light" was expounded on in the July 2013, Study edition of the Watchtower with the topic of "Who Really is the faithful and discreet slave?" The article says "Do all anointed ones on earth make up the faithful slave? No… Who, then, is the faithful and discreet slave? In keeping with Jesus' pattern of feeding many through the hands of a few, that slave is made up of *a small group of anointed brothers who are directly involved in preparing and dispensing spiritual food during Christ's presence*… In recent decades, that slave has been closely identified with the Governing Body of Jehovah's Witnesses." (Italics theirs)

This is a major change in the understanding and theology of Jehovah's Witnesses, it would be like the Catholic Church saying that the Pope is no longer God's representative, but that the Cardinals when they come together act as "Pope". It's that major of a change! Yet how are Jehovah's Witnesses reacting? The members of my family and the few Witnesses who I have contacted seem little bothered by this change. The reason for this minimal reaction from the rank and file is because of the years of conditioning by the Watchtower that anytime they introduce a change in doctrine the members are to view it as "God making the light brighter", which make the Witnesses actually welcome new "understandings".

The average Witness is mesmerized by the concept of the organization, so much so that it almost takes a life of its own. I know from experience that when I was in a conversation with another JW, anytime a reference was made to the "organization" it was almost like we were talking about a person. I really felt that the organization was in some way personal, and I genuinely believed that it was God's mouthpiece and channel and that it really had my best interest in mind. As a Witness I also believed that the organization served as my mediator between me and Jehovah God. The Watchtower actually taught that "in this strict Biblical sense Jesus is the "mediator" only for anointed Christians." (*The Watchtower*, April 1st, 1979) Thus in order for me or any other JW to "keep in relationship with "our Savior, God," the "great crowd" needs to remain united with the remnant of spiritual Israelites." (*The Watchtower*, Nov. 15, 1979)

The organization served as my channel to God, my mediator, and God's mouthpiece and authority over me. In fact, the Watchtower organization painted itself as Noah's ark and that salvation can only be found in association with this channel. "To **receive everlasting life** in the earthly Paradise we must identify that **organization** and serve God as part of it." (*The Watchtower*, February 15, 1983) It was simple for me, I had to listen and obey Jehovah's organization, his "faithful slave" in order to have God's approval. It is actually taught in the organization that "we need to **obey** the faithful and discreet slave to have **Jehovah's approval**." (*The Watchtower*, July 15, 2011) The September 15, 2010 Watchtower magazine stated: "The anointed and their other sheep companions recognize that by following the lead of the modern-day Governing Body, they are in fact following their Leader, Christ." What utter words of blasphemy!

The Watchtower in a way has set itself up in the place of Christ, for when the Witness should be looking to Jesus alone as their mediator, (1 Timothy 2:5) and be looking to Jesus alone for salvation, they look instead to the organization. It is organizational idolatry; the Watchtower Society has set itself up as an idol in the hearts and minds of Jehovah's Witnesses, and they don't even realize it.

God in reality has no need for an organization to serve as a mouthpiece or mediator. The Bible says "God, who long ago **spoke** on many occasions and **in many ways** to our forefathers by means of the prophets, has at the **end of these days spoken** to us by means of a **Son**". (Hebrews 1:1-2, NWT) No organization served in past times as God's spokesman, or in these last days; for Jehovah God has appointed his Son to be the channel of communication between man and God, not an organization. Nor does God need an organization to act as a modern day "Noah's ark", for it is written, "There is no **salvation in anyone else,** for there is not another name under heaven that **has**

been given among men by which we must get **saved**." (Acts 4:12, NWT) Jesus said "If anyone thirsts he should **come to me** and drink! The one who **believes in me**, as the Scripture says, will have streams of living water flow from deep within him". (John 7:37-38) Christians need to point Jehovah's Witnesses to Jesus as the perfect mouthpiece, mediator and source of eternal life, not an organization that constantly changes their teachings. Jesus Christ is the same yesterday, today and forever and his promises and teachings never change! (Hebrews 13:8) Jesus never said that he would establish an organization, but invited people to follow him and that those who would follow him would become members of a community of believers called the Church, or the Christian Congregation, which Christ Jesus himself is the corner stone. (Matthew 16:18; 18:20; 1 Peter 2:4-10)

Jehovah's Witnesses are putting all their faith in the men who claim to be God's "faithful slave" and even modern day "Ezekiel's" and "Jeremiah's". We need to point the JW to the Scriptures and ask them to truly test the words, history and teachings of their leaders to the never changing, inspired Word of God. (Isaiah 40:8) Jesus said to the Church in Ephesus that commended them for testing those "who say they are apostles, but they are not, and you found them liars". (Revelation 2:2, NWT) Show them that even the Berean's tested the words of the Apostle Paul and held him to the authority of the Scriptures. (Acts 17:11) The Bible warns us to put to test anyone who claims to be from Jehovah God, for many false prophets have gone into the world. (1 John 4:1) Are Jehovah's Witnesses being misled by a false prophet organization?

ARE JEHOVAH'S WITNESSES FALSE PROPHETS?

How can we identify false prophets? In the Bible book of Deuteronomy chapter 18 verse 21 we are confronted with a critical question, "And in case you should say in your heart: "How shall we know the word that Jehovah has not spoken?". Indeed, how can we as Christians and also Jehovah's Witnesses know the words God has not spoken? The history of Jehovah's Witnesses and the Watchtower Bible and Tract Society is riddled with dates, expectations and flat out false prophecies regarding the return of Jesus Christ and the "end of the world". The Society was built and founded on a foundation of lies; Charles Taze Russell taught that Jesus returned invisibly not in the year 1914, but in 1878. In his book, "Studies in the Scriptures" the fourth volume, he wrote concerning Christ return: "Our Lord, the appointed King, is **now present, since October 1874**". He also taught that 1914 would signify not the beginning of the end, but the complete end, "But bear in mind that the end of 1914 **is not the date for the beginning**, but for the **end of the time** of trouble". (*Zion's Watchtower*, July 15th, 1894) Russell also wrote in his book, "The Time is at Hand!" that "the 'battle of the great day of God Almighty' (Revelation 16:14), which **will end in A.D. 1914.**"

Even after the end came, not for the world but for Charles T Russell, his successors would continue on in the same spirit of false prophecy. Judge Rutherford, the 2nd President of the Watchtower Society claimed that "we may confidently expect that **1925 will mark the return of Abraham, Isaac, Jacob** and the faithful prophets of old", in his book "Millions Now Living Will Never Die!" During the 1960's the leaders of the Watchtower started beating the drums again, now pointing to a new date, the year 1975. The leaders of the Society started teaching that 1975 marked 6000 years of human creation and that they should expect the 1000 year reign or "Sabbath rest" of Jesus Christ. This time around the leadership heavily suggested and *implied* that 1975 would mark the end, rather than flat out declaring it in their publications. In the book "Life Everlasting in Freedom of the Sons of God", we see this discussion on 1975:

"**According to this trustworthy Bible chronology** six thousand years from man's creation will **end in** 1975, and the seventh period of a thousand years of human history will begin in the fall of 1975 C.E... **How appropriate it would be for Jehovah God to make of this coming seventh period of a thousand years a sabbath period**... It would also be most fitting on God's part, for, remember, mankind has yet ahead of it what the last book of the Holy Bible speaks of as the reign of Jesus Christ over earth for a thousand years, the millennial reign of Christ. **It would not be by mere chance or accident** but would be **according** to the loving **purpose of Jehovah God** for **the reign of Jesus Christ**, the 'Lord of the Sabbath,' to **run parallel with the seventh millennium of man's existence.**" In other words, "Wink! Wink!"

The history of the Watchtower is littered with dates and false predictions regarding the end of the world, so much so that I cannot go over every single event for time and space does not allow. So why do Jehovah's Witnesses still follow and trust the Watchtower Society as their 'mediator' and 'channel' if it has been wrong so many times? It is truly a strange thing, I can recall being confronted with some of these failed predictions on the internet, and I thought to myself, "No this is impossible, these dates and quotes are all made up by apostates. Satan is only trying to deceive me!" Yet when I would go to the library in my Kingdom Hall to verify the validity of those claims I was shocked. When I asked my mother and a few Witnesses I confided in, it was as if nothing was wrong, it was passively dismissed as a simple mistake, "old light" that Jehovah corrected. At the time, I was actually impressed with how strong their faith was that not even these old errors affected them, I thought maybe something was wrong with me. So I buried the doubts and old predictions in the back of my mind and marched on like a good Jehovah's Witness.

Eventually the more time I spent on the internet, the more I felt the need to research and confront this issue. I wanted to prove that my organization was not a false prophet, that they had merely made mistakes but that Jehovah corrected them. So I brought my defense to the internet, and began posting videos on YouTube defending my faith against the accusations that we were false prophets. The average Witness probably knows very little, if anything at all about the failed predictions of the Watchtower. Some may know just enough to not have any doubts, not really knowing the extent of the error that their organization was in. For those who were honest Jehovah's Witnesses like myself, I knew more about past predictions and doctrines than most elders in the congregation. For me it was always about being honest and seeking the truth, and because I desperately wanted my religion to be the truth and not a false prophet organization, I came up with reasoning's and defenses on behalf of the Watchtowers errors. The argument that I made as a young JW apologist was that the Society never claimed to be "inspired" in the same manner that the apostles and prophets were. I would point to quotes in the Watchtower publications where they acknowledged they were imperfect and fallible. I felt this was a perfect argument; they could not be false prophets for they never claimed to be "inspired prophets" or that they had ever "prophesied" in Jehovah's name. Or did they?

The deeper I studied Watchtower literature however, the more I began to see the holes in my own argument. In the Watchtower, the Society has claimed to act and speak as a prophet of God. "So does Jehovah have a **prophet** to help them, to warn them of dangers and to declare things to come? ... This "prophet" was not one man, but was a body of men and women. It was the small group of footstep followers of Jesus Christ, known at that time as International Bible Students. **Today** they are known as **Jehovah's Christian**

Witnesses...Of course, it is easy to say that this group acts as a 'prophet' of God. It is another thing to **prove it**". (*The Watchtower*, April 1st, 1972) Some Witnesses will say, "Yes but they never claimed to be inspired or to actually prophesy". This is a strange argument, for this organization claims to be God's "channel of communication", therefore they claim that God is communicating... Sounds like prophets and prophesying to me. The Society has even identified itself as the "Ezekiel class", the "Jeremiah class" and the "John class", identifying with these prophets as modern day counterparts. Ezekiel, Jeremiah and John were most certainly inspired prophets. Have they ever claimed to "prophesy"? In the book, "Live With Jehovah's Day In Mind" page 167 we read, "**Now consider our time**. Joel's prophecy has been undergoing its major fulfillment since early in the 20th century. **Spirit-anointed Christians**- male and female, old and young- began to "**prophesy**", that is, to declare "the magnificent things of God", including the good news of the Kingdom, now established in the heavens".

Some say that the only reason I began to doubt and to view the false prophecies of the Watchtower as something serious was because of reading "apostate literature" on the internet and communicating with "apostates". While it is true that during this time I was personally engaged with debating and responding to these issues, usually brought up by ex-JW's or Christian apologists, what did it for me was reading both old and new literature from my own organization. I was brought up to not trust any information that didn't come from my religion, so every time an accusation about my organizations history or beliefs came into question, I would always research the material in my own literature. There were so many times when I just could not go to sleep because of the things I read in my organizations literature. I tried and wanted to defend them so badly, but I began finding myself frustrated over the indefensible material that the Watchtower Society has printed over the years. Yet I had one last trick up my sleeve, the defense that every Jehovah's Witness comes prepared with, the argument of "New Light".

New light is a term used by Jehovah's Witnesses to define a new and refreshed doctrinal understanding, or in other words, when the Governing Body changes their mind on a certain teaching. This notion is based on Proverbs 4:18 which read, "But the path of the righteous ones is like the bright light that is getting lighter and lighter until the day is firmly established." In the eyes of JW's, this verse justifies every instance where their leaders see fit to change a teaching, including the cases where the Society clearly predicted the end on specific dates. Unfortunately in many cases, "new light" can also mean life or death for the Jehovah's Witness. Take for example the Watchtowers ever evolving teaching on blood transfusions and organ transplants. During the 1940's the Watchtower banned its members from taking blood transfusion, those who did would be excommunicated and lose their standing with God and Christ. Shortly afterwards they also put a ban on organ transplants, claiming that it was a form of cannibalism and that it violated God's everlasting covenant. From 15th November 1967 until 29th March 1980 the Watchtower maintained the ban on organ transplants until the Governing Body finally saw "the light" and published that organ transplants are now a "conscientious decision". But within those 13 years of the ban, the decision was already made for thousands of Jehovah's Witnesses who lost their lives because of a religious doctrine that "God's channel of communication", his John class and prophet, had wrong. This is when the pieces came together for me, when I realized that Jehovah God would never misguide his people into losing their lives for a lie. I discovered that "new light" was merely a cover up for a new lie, a fancy way for the perpetrators of these lies to get away from any responsibility of blame and in fact blame God for the misunderstanding since all spiritual "meat" or light is given in "due season" by the Creator.

In the beginning of this section, I quoted from Deuteronomy 18:21 "How shall we know the word that Jehovah has not spoken?" The answer: "when the prophet **speaks in the name of Jehovah** and the **word does not occur or come true**, that is the word that Jehovah did not speak. With **presumptuousness** the prophet spoke it. You must not get **frightened** at him.'" (Verse 22) After two years of defending the organization on YouTube and other sites, my conscience could hold no longer. What would bother me the most however is how the Society always covers up there failures like they never happened, or by blaming the members for "speculating" when it was in fact their very leaders who were the ones speculating and speaking a word that Jehovah did not command. I could no longer defend an organization with so many failed prophecies that I do not even have the time and space to write about in this book. Dates and predictions such as 1874, 1914, 1915, 1918, 1919, 1925, 1941, and 1975- all dates the Society, God's spokesman claimed would be the "end". Knowing that they were false prophets, and not God's "faithful slave" since they have *not* been faithful neither to the Scriptures or their followers, it allowed me to break free from the fear of these men. I do not believe that the sincere Witness who goes knocking door to door with his son is a false prophet, but I do believe that he is representing one. The past and present leadership and Governing Body of Jehovah's Witnesses are false prophets who are deceiving millions of Jehovah's Witnesses, for as Jesus warned, "Be on the watch for the false prophets that come to YOU in sheep's covering, but inside they are ravenous wolves." (Matthew 7:15, NWT)

The Watchtower Society is a movement that is obsessed with the end of the World, and it was an organization that was not meant to be around this long. The whole premise of this religion has been the that end is near, thus why they have always been obsessed with setting dates, and every month, year and decade that passes and the "end" hasn't arrived, the closer we are actually getting to the end of the Watchtower Society. Just consider this, the organization teaches that the "end times" began in 1914, and here we are on the verge of 2014, 100 years since the end times began, yet we are all still here. Many Witnesses are beginning to see that the foundation of their 1914 message is faulty at best. But how can you practically use this information to help the Witnesses break free?

If you even try to bring up the history of the Watchtower or their false prophecies the Witnesses will become very defensive and suspicious of you. They will assume you've read "apostate" information and maybe that Satan is using you to weaken their faith. If you want to help a Witness think critically of their own organizations failed predictions, put things into perspective by using examples other than the Watchtower. For example, a fringe preacher named Harold Camping made big headlines a few years back for his claim that God would bring judgment day on May 21st, 2011. He gained a massive following, with his people selling all their possessions and going around the country proclaiming this coming judgment. Sound familiar? When May 21st, 2011 came and went, Mr. Camping was exposed to the world as a false prophet, and what did he do? He went on to say that he made a mistake that the end is really going to be on October 21st of 2011. When that prediction failed, he told his followers that a "spiritual" judgment had come and not a physical one. Again, sound familiar? As this was all over the news I heard my mother talking about how the guy was crazy and that he was a false prophet. I used that opportunity to ask her, "So if someone claims to have a message from God and predict the end and it does not occur, are they false prophets?" She responded, "Of course! The Bible warns us that false prophets would arise in the last days". I said, "I'm glad we can agree on that, I too believe that this man is a false prophet because he proclaimed something that did not occur. Mom, you got baptized in 1975, what were the expectations surrounding that date?" As you can probably imagine, the conversation didn't get too far, but it's because my knows my stance and knew where I was heading. With any other Witness I believe an approach that puts things into perspective where they can examine an almost exact mirror problem that another religion or sect faces will have much fruit.

At the end of the day however, will any of this help a Jehovah's Witness? Perhaps. Many feel that the best way to wake up a Jehovah's Witness is by shocking them with all of the unfulfilled prophecies made by the Watchtower, or showing them how their teachings have changed over the years. If you believe that by force feeding a Witness unfulfilled dates and predictions from their past will set them free, you are mistaken. The amount of shock that I received slowly unraveling these things were devastating to my faith. It took me over 2 years of examining the facts to finally stand up for what was true, and for some JW's it may take a lifetime. You can certainly lead a Witness out of the Watchtower by providing enough material on their constantly evolving doctrines masquerading as "New Light", or by showing enough quotations of their own literature showing the Watchtower predicted the end of the World multiple times, but then what? Are those things important? Absolutely, but the Witness will ask "If the Jehovah Witnesses are not the Truth, then what is the truth?" Jesus said "Therefore if the Son sets YOU free, YOU will be actually free."(John 8:36 NWT) And "I am the way and the truth and the life. No one comes to the Father except through me." (John 14:6, NWT)

Our goal is not to destroy their faith or to direct them to another religion or organization. Our goal is to lead them to the Person of Truth, the One who sets all man free, Jesus Christ himself. Men and religion will always let mankind down, and when the Witness comes face to face with the reality that they have been following a false prophet organization, only Jesus can take a broken and confused soul and make out of him a "new creation". (2 Corinthians 5:17)

CHAPTER 7

GIVING A WITNESS TO JEHOVAH'S WITNESSES

K nock, knock… I often run into Christians who hear about my story and tell me about how fast they have been to dismiss the Jehovah's Witnesses who come knocking on their door. I often hear about how Christians have prayed that the Jehovah's Witnesses and Mormons would just not ever knock on their doors. When I hear these words come out of the mouth of Christians, it breaks my heart. What in effect I hear them telling me is this, "If your Witness family members came knocking on my door, I would just pray them away!" Pray them away? I have met countless Christian believers who have told me that when Jehovah's Witnesses have come knocking they simply turned down any conversation.

Hey I get it, witnessing to a Jehovah's Witness is not exactly what you expected to do on a Saturday morning, and it certainly is not the easiest thing to do either. But what would Jesus do? Better yet, what does Christ tell us to do? What ever happened to letting our light shine before men, and giving everyone a reason for the hope within? What has happened to the Church, the fortress of the truth?

When I was in the door to door ministry as a JW, I would come across professing Christian that had just come out of church services that were either totally uninterested in discussing the Bible with us, or didn't have a clue as to what they were talking about. They're were countless times when I would approach a door and have the person answer "We are Christians and already believe in God here!" followed by a slammed door to the face. This type of action reinforced my conviction as a Witness and made it easy for me and other JW's to begin our deconstruction of "Christendom's" belief system and lay flat what they believed. I was convinced that the churches were spiritually bankrupt and produced "church goers" who knew absolutely nothing about the Bible. In my mind, Christendom's 'fruit' was rotten, while our Kingdom Halls were filled with people who knew and wanted to share the Bible. Secretly, however I always wanted to meet a Christian with a set of convictions, someone who was not afraid to share their faith with me, a Jehovah's Witness.

Many Christians are afraid to engage with JW's because they feel overwhelmed or underprepared to speak with Witnesses. They feel like speaking to a JW will only end in fruitless debates and arguments. Many Christians lack the confidence or simply the desires to witness to a JW, I've heard of countless people tell me they were intimidated by the Witnesses confidence in their beliefs. If this is how you feel, let me tell you that when I would engage in the door to door ministry as a JW I would outwardly seem to have composure and complete assurance in my beliefs, I seemed to have all the answers and have it all together. I had all my lines ready for when they opened the door, but inwardly I was lost and hungry for God. Keep in mind that when a Witness knocks on your door, they may outwardly seem to have all the answers in the world, but inwardly they are without Christ and are in need of grace and freedom. I can testify that in my own life as a Witness I was in desperate need of grace, and in desperate need of Jesus.

I personally believe that the reason we don't have many Christians witnessing to JW's is because todays Christians lack conviction. I encountered so many so-called Christians as a Witness that lacked the conviction and grace to share Jesus with me. Here I was, standing at their door steps, at the door steps of Pastors, deacons, choir singers and church goers, and not once in 16 years did anyone to my recollection invite me in to share their faith. I often think and wonder of my mother, how different things would be if someone just gave a witness! I pray daily that God would send her a witness, and I still hope that as she goes knocking on doors that a Christian with conviction would open that door and sit her down and show her Jesus, for she refuses to speak to me about Him.

As you begin to understand a Jehovah's Witness you will begin to realize how difficult it is to approach sharing your faith with a Witness. It is no easy task giving a witness to a JW, for often time the conversation between a Christian and a Witness is marred with debates regarding Christ divinity, the existence or lack thereof of Hell, Heaven and the 144,000, or the Trinity with the Jehovah's Witness often time pretty comfortably attempting to debunk everything you believe. What can *you* do when Jehovah's Witnesses come knocking on your door? What approach is most effective in dealing with the Witness at the door? The first and most important thing to always remember when encountering a JW is that behind their zeal and outwardly impressive knowledge of the Scriptures, they are in fact just as in need of Jesus and grace as anyone else we minister to in the streets or our churches.

BE PREPARED, BE A BEREAN.

No one knows more than I do how difficult it is to witness to a Jehovah's Witness, because I lived it. Witnessing to a JW is a very difficult task and to effectively minister to them you need to be prepared. Keep in mind that you will become frustrated, you will become tired, you will become challenged, and you may never even see immediate fruit. Too many Christians may not understand how to approach witnessing to a Jehovah's Witness when they come knocking at your door step. The Apostle Peter gives us some clarity on the issue where he urges Christians to "sanctify Christ as Lord in your hearts, **always being ready to make a defense** to everyone who asks you to give an account for the hope that is in you, yet with **gentleness and reverence**". (1 Peter 3:15 NASB) Believers are called to sanctify or set apart Christ as Lord in and by their act of giving a defense, or literally an "answer" (Greek: apologia) to everyone who demands one. Dear Christian you are called to defend, proclaim, and give an answer for the Gospel by which you have been saved. The very act of 'apologia' or giving a defense is in fact bringing honor to Christ. This does not necessarily mean we must know the ins and outs of every religious group that opposes Christ, but it calls us to know why we believe what we believe. The Jehovah's Witness does not necessarily know what you believe, but they sure do know what *they* believe. Therefore, if you want to lay the ground work to witnessing to JW's or anyone else for that matter, than know your Bible and know your Savior. Also realize, not every topic from Hell to the eternal nature of the soul, or blood transfusions are worth picking a fight and arguing over. Major in the majors as they say, and minor on the minors. Sure those things are worth discussing, but it's not worth losing the opportunity to share Christ with them. Have gentleness and reverence as you share Christ message.

I can assure you that when a JW encounters someone who has conviction, someone who is prepared with an answer for the hope that is within them, they take notice. One way we can practically be prepared for encountering JW's is to have realistic expectations of your witnessing to them. Surely we know that with God all things are possible, but it is important to have a level head and understand that chances of you converting and leading a JW in prayer to receive Christ on their first visit to your doorstep is unrealistic. You may never even see a JW whom you have ministered to come to faith in Christ. You will encounter road blocks; you will become frustrated and tired. Our intent with any opportunity we have to speak with a JW especially in our initial contact with them is to plant seeds, not seeds of doubt, but seeds of faith in Jesus. The JW may be impressed or even delighted to see that you are interested in God and know your Bible, but often time some Christians become overzealous in their approach to the JW's and actually turn them away from ever coming back.

For example, when I was defending the Watchtower Society on the Internet, I would get messages from "Born again" believers who would mock and be condescending toward me and my beliefs by calling me "blind" and a part of a "false prophet" religion. They would send me messages filled with contradictions in Watchtower theology and quotes from the publications showing that they predicted the end of the world numerous times. But did any of those messages actually help me? Not one bit. Many of those messages and interactions may have been well intended, but they were trying to simply "debunk" my faith and not actually point me to Christ. I actually considered many messages from Christians as 'attacks' and use it as fuel to strengthen my conviction that I was a part of God's one true religion.

So that was an example of Christians who knew a lot about Jehovah's Witnesses, but little fruit resulted in their efforts, what was missing? These Christians apologist gave me answers, but it was not answers for "the hope" that is within Christ. (1 Peter 3:15) How we present the Gospel matters. The World tends to view Christians as extreme "right wing" fundamentalist holding signs up proclaiming certain people groups are going to Hell. As a Witness this is how I viewed the Christians trying to debunk my faith and who were trying to convert me. I felt as if they were mean spirited or just looking for an argument. What was missing from their messages was love. The Apostle Paul said that if he could speak in the tongues of Angels yet not have love, then the words coming from his mouth is just clanging noise. He said that he could have all the knowledge and know all the mysteries of the faith, but if did not have love he had nothing. (1 Corinthians 13:1-2) If you want to reach out to a Jehovah's Witness, Love them. Dear Christian, if you want to reach your relatives, friends, culture and World with the Gospel, have love. Truth delivered by Love is the Kingdom way to reach the hearts of the unsaved, for ignorance and arrogance will not convict anyone of their error, only the work of the Holy Spirit working through love can accomplish it.

But merely showing love by itself is not sufficient, you need to let the Witness know that the Bible is your final authority and that you are a Berean who will examine their words and teachings by the light of Scripture. In Acts 17:11 Paul commended those in Berea and said they were more noble-minded for examining the words of Paul to the Holy Scriptures. The Berean's did not take Paul's words at face value; they tested him to see if his words lined up with the Word of God. Likewise, we want to tell the JW's that we are Berean Christians and encourage them to have the same spirit and eager-ness to examine the Scriptures as the Berean's.

THINGS TO KEEP IN MIND

Probably the most important thing I can tell you regarding reaching out to Jehovah's Witnesses is this; the Witness you encounter is conditioned against you. What do I mean? Jehovah's Witnesses on average attend two meetings a week, spend at least 10 hours of field ministry or door to door work, and they have been taught and indoctrinated to view anyone who tries to witness to them as enemies of the truth, and they immediately shut off. Irony? Through mind control tactics, the Watchtower has made their Witnesses immune to outside teaching. So how can we get through to them?

Remember that when speaking with anyone of a different world and reli-gious view always try and find common ground. Be intentional and sincere in establishing common ground, especially with Jehovah's Witnesses. The great thing is the JW's have also been taught to search for common ground with those whom they engage with. As they establish their love and trust in the Bible as the Word of God, they will then look for an open door to smuggle the difference they no doubt share with you, and trust me there are a lot!

When interacting with a JW, as with any other person, first impressions matter. The Witnesses are taught to seek out "rightly disposed" individuals who will respond favorably to the message. If the JW feels at all threatened or antagonized they will likely not return the visit. The JW's love having command over the conversations at the door, especially if they see that you know your Bible. Remember, the Witnesses are not accustomed to interacting with Christians who know their Bible. So what can you do to ensure that they return after your initial contact? Ask plenty of good, sincere questions! The Witnesses love to answer people's questions; they believe that they are at your door step or on the Street corner passing out literature to help educate you and your neighbors about the Bible. Since they believe they are there to help you, let them help! And for the sake of honesty and integrity, let them know that you are a person of strong Christian convictions and that you are not necessarily interested in becoming a Jehovah's Witness, but let them know that you do have a lot of questions. They will respect your honesty, and more than likely will return the visit with the hope of swaying you to their side.

Be tactful in your interactions with them, remember that they are there for one reason and that is to ultimately convert you to the Watchtower. The Witness is trained to disengage from people who are not receptive to their message. We need to contend in a tactful manner; Jesus said we ought to "be wise as serpents and innocent as doves." (Matthew 10:16) Therefore in your first contact with a Jehovah's Witness, do not be overly combative, ask questions and invite dialogue. The JW's will definitely return to answer any questions that you have, but bear in mind that during the course of your discussions the Witness will impose one of their teaching books, such as the book "What Does the Bible *Really* Teach?", and ask you if you'd be interested in starting a free home "Bible study" with them. This will now be up to you, whether you want to get stuck in a tedious weekly book study with the Witness, or kindly decline and ask if you can merely talk about the Scriptures without the help of any aids. Chances are after a few sessions with the JW's, they will give you the ultimatum of continuing your discussions by submitting to one of their book studies, or no longer come and meet with you. Your job, dear Christian is to give the Jehovah's Witness as much of the Gospel of Jesus Christ as the Holy Spirit allows you to. If you decide to meet with Jehovah's Witnesses, be in deep fervent prayer; pray that the Holy Spirit would enlighten you with the truth of the Scriptures, and that he would equip you to give a witness to the Jehovah's Witness. Prayer and study of God's Word cannot be over stated in your pursuit to win over a JW for Jesus Christ.

Try and maintain just one topic per discussion, for Witnesses love taking you all over the Bible and talk about various topics at once in efforts to overwhelm you with their knowledge. Prepare yourself with a set of questions that are all related to one topic, for example their teaching that Jesus is Michael the Archangel. Tell them you heard that they believe that Christ and Michael are one in the same and that you had some questions pertaining to that one topic. You could ask them how they reconcile that teaching with the teaching received in the 1ˢᵗ Chapter of the Book of Hebrews, which teaches that Christ is not a created Angel but the Creator. You can raise any topic you feel ready to engage in, but make sure that they do not deviate from that one topic. If they do begin to go on a tirade on a topic foreign to the discussion, politely decline speaking about it until your answers on the topic at hand are answered. You will be more effective in witnessing to them if you stick to one topic per discussion for it forces them to think about the verses and questions at hand. The best thing to do is not to overwhelm the Witness with what you know, but to simply get them to think about an important Bible verse or topic that is opposed to their system of thought.

Another essential thing to remember when witnessing to a Jehovah's Witness is that they are sincerely wrong people. They sincerely believe that what they teach is the truth and that they are quite literally doing the Lord's work. Do not forget that behind the suit or dress, behind the Watchtower and Awake magazines, and behind all their arguments for their Organization there is a human being in need of the grace and salvation of Jesus Christ. When I was a Witness I would always come across as confident and maybe even a little snug, brandishing my Bible knowledge to others at the door, but inwardly I was exhausted and spiritually unfulfilled. I was "always learning and never able to come to a knowledge of the truth." (2 Timothy 3:7; HCSB) In your ministering to a Jehovah's Witness do not be discouraged if you do not see immediate fruit from your discussions with them. They've been trained on how to handle every situation, even how to keep cool when faced with a challenging set of questions. Even if they seem totally composed, inwardly they may be asking themselves very serious questions regarding their beliefs. This was the case with me when asked convicting questions by those whom I interacted with online.

BE A SERVANT TEACHER

This may be the most difficult approach when interacting with Jehovah's Witnesses; being a Servant Teacher. What do I mean? It can be very tempting to just get in long drawn out debates over doctrines and belief systems. We don't want that. The Apostle Paul wrote to Timothy "Remind them of these things, charging them before God not to fight about words; **this is in no way profitable and leads to the ruin of the hearers**. Be diligent to present yourself approved to God, a worker who doesn't need to be ashamed, *correctly teaching the word of truth*." (2 Timothy 2:14-15 HCSB) Therefore it is important to realize that our giving a defense for the hope is no excuse for fruitless debates, for you can very well win an argument but you should not be interested in winning debates rather you should be interested in winning hearts! We want to act in such a way that the Jehovah's Witness will want to continue talking to us; we want to walk in truth and humility. Remember, the JW is at your door step to help *you* understand the Bible, in their minds they are the Teachers, not you, no matter how much you may know your Bible. The average JW actually believes that they know more about the truth of the Bible, than any Pastor, Preacher, or Theologian in Christendom. Therefore if you take the approach of trying to dominate the conversations and teach over the Witnesses, chances are they will leave faster than a knock on the door.

Paul urged Timothy not to partake in fruitless debates, for often time they do not build up rather they lead to the ruin of its hearers. We need to be diligent students of God's Word, correctly handling and teaching the truth of Jesus to the Jehovah's Witness. Instead of focusing our energies on debating Theology with the Witness, we ought to focus on the actual person. If possible try to get to know the JW personally, ask them about their families, their work, how they became JW's. This will humanize your discussions with the Witnesses. You won't simply view the Witness as a lost Cult member but as a human being, and the Witness will not look at you as just a lost potential convert but as an individual. Let them know that you are interested in asking them questions with the intent of understanding them better, not necessarily because you are interested in converting to their religion. Establishing the fact that you are interested in their beliefs yet unwavering in your own will set a mutual tone for your meetings with the Witnesses.

Politely tell them that you would be delighted to have a discussion about the Bible and that you would love to use this time to inform them about your beliefs as they inform you about their beliefs. The Witness will often time want to know where you stand in a certain doctrinal issue, which then may become an opportunity for you to share the convictions of your heart as laid out in Scripture. Use those opportunities wisely, for when your doctrines disagree, and they will, the Witness will go on the attack and once they do it is vital that you level the conversation and urge them that you agreed to talk mutually about the Bible. Often time the JW's will try and dominate the conversation and try to dismantle all of the 'contradictions' in Christendom, while boastfully heralding their teachings as "the truth". Let the JW feel as if he is doing his role in teaching, be a Servant by means of listening to what they have to say, and be a Teacher in the manner you ask challenging and convicting questions. Be patient and ask God to open opportunities and doors for the Witness to receive the ultimate witness of Jesus Christ and his redeeming love for them.

Unfortunately none of this will guarantee that a Jehovah's Witness will come to know Christ, but the witness of Jesus must be given regardless if they accept it. If every Christian took the Great Commission of Jesus Christ to go and make disciples as serious as the Jehovah Witnesses have, then not only would there be less people involved in the Watchtower or Mormonism, but the World as we know it would be forever changed by the transforming message that only we possess. So what are you waiting for? Can I get a witness?

CHAPTER 8

THE JESUS OF THE WATCHTOWER

I was 13 years old, standing before a crowd of thousands of Jehovah's Witnesses, my legs numb as they asked me and others this question; "On the basis of the sacrifice of Jesus Christ, have you repented of your sins and dedicated yourself to Jehovah to do his will?"

I responded with the others in a resounding, "Yes!" This was one of two questions asked before my baptism as one of Jehovah's Witnesses.

At this tender age I dedicated myself to God in water baptism, confessing before many Witnesses (literally) that my life now belonged to God through Christ. However deep down inside I felt that I had a shallow and superficial relationship with Christ. I was taught that it was Jehovah I needed to have a relationship with, Jesus was simply the middle man. Although young, I understood a lot about God as Father, and I knew that Jesus played a vital role in Jehovah's purpose. I had knowledge. But did I have Jesus? Or even a better question, which Jesus did I have?

A Bible verse almost universally known by Jehovah's Witnesses in John 17:3 which Read as follows in the NWT: "This means everlasting life, their taking in knowledge of you, the only true God, and of the one whom you sent forth, Jesus Christ." They point to this verse to potential converts and share it regularly at their meetings. They claim that one must 'take in knowledge' of Jesus and Jehovah, as distinct beings in order to have the prospect of eternal life. They say that it even disqualifies Jesus from being God.

Some however have had the misconception that Jehovah's Witnesses do not believe in Jesus Christ. The Witness will zealously refute that and explain that they very much do believe in Jesus Christ. In fact to them Jesus is the Son of God! Surely a Christian should be able to examine the claim of any religious organization that comes to them bearing the name of Christ in order to give a ready defense for the gospel. (1 Peter 3:15) No topic is as imperative in dealing with Jehovah's Witnesses and anybody else for that matter, then the topic of our Lord, Jesus Christ.

But I don't merely want to just tell you **what** the JW's believe in regarding Christ, but I want to tell you **why** they believe it. In this chapter I want to help you understand the JW stance on Jesus, and give you the view point of a former Jehovah's Witness apologist. In the coming chapters we will unravel together the Jesus according to the Watchtower and the Jesus of the Bible.

Jesus of the Watchtower- "a god"

If there was one thing I knew crystal clear about Jesus growing up JW, it was that Jesus was not God but the Son of God. In the book "The Greatest Man who ever lived" published by Jehovah Witnesses, it says this concerning Jesus: "Jesus **never claimed to be God**, but he acknowledged that he was the promised Messiah, or Christ. **He also said he was "God's Son", not God**. Yet, the Bible does not say Jesus was a man like any other man. He was a very special because he was *created* by God **before all other things**." (Emphasis mine)

Jehovah's Witnesses are quick to make the distinction between Jesus not being God but the Son of God. The Witness believes that the reason Jesus is called "the Son of God" is because they believe Jesus was directly created by God the Father and by virtue of being created directly by the Father, Jesus is called the "only-begotten" Son of God. They point to such verses as Colossians 1:15, Revelation 3:14, John 3:16 to justify their argument. Witnesses teach that Jesus enjoyed a pre-human existence with the Father,

Jehovah, and that by means of Jesus, Jehovah God created the cosmos, or all "other things".(Colossians 1:16, NWT)

Since Jesus is called the "firstborn of all creation" and the "beginning of the creation by God", clearly then Jesus has a beginning, the Witness will argue. The Watchtower also takes Proverbs 8:22-31 and apply it to the pre-incarnate Christ, arguing that Jesus is Wisdom personified when Wisdom proclaims, "Jehovah himself produced me as the beginning of his way, the earliest of his achievements of long ago". An interesting argument is hence brought forth that usually leaves the Christian on the other side scratching their heads.

I use to enjoy stumping people and opponents at the door or on the internet forums with such Bible verses. At the Kingdom Hall we were trained to answer various objections that could possibly arise at the door, and thus we mastered the art of playing 'Bible hop scotch', taking one isolated verse and applying it to another to make our point. The experienced Witnesses can debate confidently from the door to the average Trinitarian and defend the Watchtowers version of Jesus. I was one of them and I loved to bring up our "Bible proof texts" to disprove what the Watchtower refers to as 'doctrines of demons'. In my mind the teaching I grew up in made sense, for instance I knew growing up that I was not the same person as my father and I knew my father greater than I was. With that in mind I could see how Jesus was God's Son according to the Watchtower.

The Watchtower points out verses in which Jesus addressed the Father in prayer and asks the question, "Who did Jesus pray to? Was he praying to Himself if he was God?" This is a favorite argument by JW's; it is an almost immediate first line of defense against those who believe Jesus is God. The Witness is then quick to show you verses like John 20:17 which Jesus says "I am ascending to my Father and YOUR Father and to my God and YOUR God" to make the point that Jesus has a God and it is the Father. In prayer Jesus even referred to the Father as "the only true God" in John 17:3, and even going as so far to say that "the Father is greater than I" in John 14:28. I didn't understand how anyone could believe that Jesus was God, when I could see so clearly that Jesus had a head above him, the Father. (1 Corinthians 11:3)

We were taught to view Jesus with respect, as he was the firstborn Son of Jehovah, and now ruling as King of God's Kingdom. But he was far from ever receiving our prayers or worship. The reasoning behind that is that since Jesus himself worshiped the Father and addressed prayers to the Father, then we also had to worship and pray to the Father in Jesus name. Jesus himself said that the true worshipers would worship the Father. (John 4:24)

Jesus is also the "Word"; he is not God but **a god,** just as judges, kings, and even Satan are all called **gods.** (John 1:1, NWT; Psalm 82:6; 2 Corinthians 4:4) I would say that Jesus could rightfully be referred to as a god, but not as Almighty God, for only one person can hold that title and position, the Father.

The Jehovah's Witnesses are well-known for their Bible's translation of John 1:1. In the New World Translation it reads, "In the beginning the Word was, and the Word was with God, and the Word was *a god."* (Emphasis mine) The Watchtower points out that in the original language the first Greek noun for God, *Theos,* is accompanied with a Greek definite article, 'the' or *Ton* in the Greek, thus when the noun for God (Theos) is used in relation to "the Word" there is no definite article, implying that the indefinite article "a" can rightfully appear. This play of linguistic trickery used by the Watchtower Society is neither honest nor Scholarly.

First, it is important to note that there is virtually no Greek New Testament Scholar, either Christian or non-Christian that agrees with the Watchtower Society's translation of John 1:1. If in the original Greek text the early Christians understood John 1:1 to mean that Christ was "a god" then why did the early Church fathers use John 1:1 in defending the deity of Christ?

The Watchtower correctly points out in their brochure, "Should You Believe in the Trinity?" page 27 that, "The Koine Greek language had a definite article ("the"), **but it did not have an indefinite article** ("a" or "an"). So when a predicate noun is not preceded by the definite article, it may be indefinite, **depending on the context."** What is interesting to note, in John 1:6 we see another instance where the Greek word for God, *Theos,* is used without a definite article. The same occurrence happens in John 1:18 in both instances in reference to the Father, yet the Watchtower was not consistent with its own Translation philosophy, and did not insert the indefinite article, "a" into the text. The Watchtower claims they based their translation of "a god" with the greater context of the rest of the Bible. They explain:

"So John 1:1 **highlights the quality of the Word,** that he was "divine", "godlike", "a god", but not Almighty God. **This harmonizes with the rest of the Bible,** which shows that Jesus, here called "the Word" in his role as God's Spokesman, was an obedient subordinate sent to earth by his Superior,

Almighty God... since John 1:1 shows that the Word was with God, he could not be God but was "a god", or "divine"." (*Should You Believe in the Trinity?*)

The Watchtower fails to take into account the Historical and Biblical understanding that Christian have had on the Trinity, the fact that "the Word was with God" shows the unity and diversity of the relation between the eternal Son and the eternal Father. The Watchtower feels it is their right to interpret Scripture and dictate what the ancients who wrote those words down actually meant. The Witnesses claim to believe in One God, yet declare Jesus to be "a god". It is Jehovah-Yahweh himself who declares, "I am Yahweh, **and there is no other; there is no God but me**". (Isaiah 45:5) And "before me there was no God formed, neither shall there be after me". (Isaiah 43:10 NWT) An excellent question to help Jehovah's Witness would be to ask them, "If Jehovah said that there would be no god formed after him, then why do you claim that Jesus was a god, formed after Jehovah?"

Another question that could be raised is "If you say that Jesus is merely "a god" like Satan is a god, A) Are you equating the god-ship of Jesus to that of Satan the Devil, and B) If Jesus is a god, is he a true God or a false God?". The truth is their translation of John 1:1 invites polytheism, an idea totally foreign to the beliefs of those in the Old and New Testament. It is not in harmony with the rest of Scripture; in fact it contradicts Scripture and dishonors Jehovah.

JESUS THE ARCHANGEL?

Jesus is the first angelic creature, Michael the archangel according to the Watchtower. In the April 1ˢᵗ, 2010 Watchtower magazine, a question is raised, "Is Jesus the Archangel Michael?" The article says: "Put simply, the answer is yes... **Michael the archangel is Jesus in his pre-human existence**. After his resurrection and return to heaven, **Jesus resumed his service as Michael, the chief angel, "to the glory of God the Father."**-Philippians 2:11" (Emphasis mine)

The JW believes that they have Scriptural reason to believe that Jesus is Michael, for example in 1 Thessalonians 4:16 Christ is said to descend from Heaven with the "voice of the archangel", and only Michael is said to be an archangel in Jude 9, therefore Jesus is Michael the Archangel. So before coming to earth Jesus was referred to by his heavenly or angelic title, Michael, which means in the Hebrew "Who is like God?" The Watchtower teaches that at his coming to earth as a man he left behind his divine or angelic nature and became Jesus of Nazareth, a perfect human with no divine nature; he was just a man. Upon his death Jehovah God resurrected Him as a spirit creature, thus becoming Michael the Archangel once again. According to JW theology, Jesus now sits enthroned in Heaven as an exalted Angel, so in effect Michael the Archangel is now sitting at God's right hand. The JW may also try to link Jesus and Michael with Revelation 12:7-9 by pointing out that Michael fights the Devil and is leader of the Lord's army; therefore Jesus must be Michael because Jesus is the one who tramples over the Devil and Jesus is the leader of the Angels and its armies.

However these notions of Jesus being Michael presents a theological and Biblical inconsistency, if Jesus and Michael is the same person, and then why not pray in the name of "Michael" since He is Jesus? If Jesus is Michael than Michael has the name "above every other name", and Michael is the long awaited Messiah and Savior. Yet we never see the Scriptures ascribe such titles to Michael the Archangel. What should be of great concern is the tactic that we see the Watchtower employ in quotations such as the one above from the April 1st, 2010 Watchtower, where they subtly deny and substitute the Lordship of Jesus Christ, destroying the context of Philippians 2:5-11 and diminishing the status of Christ to equate him with Michael the Archangel, "to the glory of God the Father". Such deceitful trickery and play on words is dishonoring to the integrity of the Scriptures, and the reality of the Lordship of Christ.

In attempting to prove their doctrine the Watchtower try's to connect vague, unrelated verses and force a meaning into them that is in itself foreign to the Scriptures. Interestingly enough this teaching is so vague that when the Watchtower publications or even the Witnesses themselves mention it, they do so in a manner that is quick and hardly ever brought up for serious discussion or study. You were expected to believe it not because you came to that conclusion yourself through a straight forward reading of the Bible, but because the Watchtower told you to believe it was true. I feel as if the average Witness will feel comfortable with any statement or teaching coming from the Watchtower as long as they put a verse or two at the end of the sentence to justify their belief. As a faithful Witness, I certainly did believe that Jesus was Michael; it didn't necessarily make sense to me, but it didn't have to. This is one of those doctrines that JW's blindly accept because they trust their leaders.

If pushed, I felt that I could make a compelling argument for Jesus being Michael; I could even win the debate against someone who believed otherwise. But I don't think there was ever a time when I felt complete conviction on the matter, it wasn't a matter many JW's spent too much time worrying or thinking about. It was a teaching that was never expounded much upon and was rarely mentioned, but yet we all knew and accepted it as 'truth'. However the teaching never sat right to me, I wanted to believe and did believe it was true, but I wanted solid evidence for believing Jesus was an Angel. In fact it would always bother me when I would hear brothers from the podium refer to Jesus as an Angel, or as Michael although that was seldom.

The Watchtower does not just stop at calling Jesus Michael the Archangel, the Society has also linked Christ Jesus as Abaddon, the Angel of the abyss in Revelation 9:6 and with the "mighty angel" of John's vision in Revelation chapter 10. In recent years the Watchtower Society has even gone as far as actually depicting artist renditions of Jesus with Angelic wings.

For further in-depth examination of the Biblical inconsistencies of this teaching go to Chapter 6 under "Jesus- "Superior than the Angels"".

ANOTHER JESUS

The Jesus of the Watchtower is a different Jesus, a Jesus the Apostles never knew, a Jesus foreign to the Scriptures, a Jesus Paul wrote about in 2 Corinthians 11:3, 4 "But I fear that, as the serpent deceived Eve **by his cunning**, your minds **may be seduced from a complete and pure devotion to Christ.** For if a person comes and **preaches another Jesus**, whom we did not preach, or you receive a different spirit, which you had not received, or a different gospel, which you had not accepted, you put up with it splendidly!"

If the teachings of Jehovah's Witnesses regarding Christ alarm you, you are not alone. Keep in mind the Witness has been trained to communicate these things subtly making them sound as "Christian" as possible. Also they will provide an abundance of proof texts to back up their claims with the Bible. Let me tell you what the Jehovah Witness at your door will tell you:

"Jehovah's Witnesses believe that Jesus is the Jewish Messiah, that he was and is the promised One foretold in the Hebrew Scriptures. We believe he was born of a virgin through the Holy Spirit, that at his incarnation he was devoid of all divinity and was just a man. We believe that Jesus lived a perfect life to set us an example for us to follow and to provide his perfect life as a Ransom to open the door to reverse what was done by the first Adam. We also believe that he is the Savior, the Son of God, and is now ruling as King of God's Kingdom, that by "taking in knowledge" of both Jesus Christ and Jehovah God one can come to have the hope of everlasting life under his Kingdom in a paradise earth."

Doesn't sound as strange now does it? Presentation is everything, and JW's have mastered the art. A lot of that we can all probably agree with, Jesus certainly is the Messiah (John 4:25, 26) he certainly was born of a Virgin birth (Matthew 1:18-23) he certainly did give his life as a Ransom for many (Matthew 20:28). Certainly there are areas in which we can agree on, and when talking with a Witness it is always wise to emphasize what we share in common. When the Witness knocks at your door, they are seeking to inform you of the "truth" of the Bible. They believe that they alone have the truth regarding Jesus and Jehovah, and they wish to help you understand the Bible. Do not be deceived, the Watchtower presents a very different Jesus than the one presented to us in the Scriptures.

Everything about the Jesus of the Watchtower is different than the Jesus of the Scriptures. The Watchtower has taken every major doctrine regarding Christ and demoted him. While the Scriptures acknowledge Jesus as the Creator, (John 1:1-3; Colossians 1:16) the Watchtower says he was just a "helper". While the Scriptures teach that Jesus was God manifested in the flesh, (John 1:1-14; John 5:18-23; Mark 2:5-10) the Watchtower says that he was just a human, devoid of all divinity. The Watchtower claims that Jesus died on a single beamed "torture stake", and that the Cross is a pagan symbol. The Gospels are clear that Jesus died on a two beamed cross, having the sign above his head not his hands, and having the use of multiple nails in his hands. (Matthew 27:37; John 20:25) The Watchtower teaches that Jesus was resurrected or recreated as a spirit creature, and that his earthly body was destroyed forever. The Bible states that Jesus died, was buried and rose again physically on the 3rd day. (Luke 24:39; Acts 13:30-37)

They have a different Jesus, a Jesus that is not supreme over all things, a Jesus that is merely "a god", a created angel. They do not believe that Jesus is the name above all names, or that Jesus is Sufficient for the complete salvation of the Jehovah's Witness.

The Jesus of the Watchtower is a Jesus that cannot save, for there is no mere man or angel that can possibly ever atone for the sins of mankind. (Psalm 49:7-15) The Watchtower Jesus falls incredibly short of the Jesus we see in the Holy Bible, however millions of Jehovah's Witnesses believe that theirs is the true Jesus of the Bible. I was one of them, but as I began to read my Bible independently of the Watchtower I began to make discoveries that would change and shape the rest of my life.

Jesus Christ in Watchtower Theology...

- Created as the "Word" or Michael the Archangel by the Father before all other things, before helping Jehovah to make to the Heavens and the Earth.

- Was born or incarnated by God's active force, the Holy Spirit as a human, devoid of all divinity and was not the Christ or Messiah until baptism by John the Baptist.

- Jesus was not God in the flesh, but was just "a god" just as Satan is 'a god'. He is the Son of God, lesser then the Father in every way.

- Jesus Christ died not upon a Cross, but a one beamed "torture stake", and was dead in a nonexistent state for three days.

- When Jesus was resurrected, he was literally recreated from the memory of God as a "spirit creature", the body that hung on the torture stake was destroyed forever.

- Jesus resumed his position as Michael the archangel, and after his ascension sat down at God's right hand.

CHAPTER 9

UNRAVELING JESUS CHRIST

Who do you say that I am?

Let's take a step into the past. Rumors are beginning to engulf the Roman occupied land of Israel, whispers of this man from Nazareth is spreading like wild fire amongst the poor and the hopeful. They say that this man heals the sick, feeds the multitudes, casts out demons, frees the oppressed, raises the dead, walks on water, and preaches the Kingdom of God, calls out the religious hypocrites, does miracles on the Sabbath. Who is this man? The most soul penetrating question of all human history still rings in the mind of all who hear of this man. The One of whom all these whispers and rumors are based upon turns and asks his disciples, "Who do people say that the Son of Man is?"

His disciples without doubt or hesitation knowing the words floating around the Empire answer in this fashion, "Some say John the Baptist; others, Elijah; still others, Jeremiah or one of the prophets."

All decent guesses, they knew something was up; something was unique with this man from Nazareth. Could he be the coming of Elijah or John the

Baptist? Was he one of the Prophets? He glances once again to his disciples and poses an even greater question to the ones who know Him best. "Who do you say that I am"? Well... who do *you* say that He is? The answer can literally mean Life or Death, the difference between eternal blessing and eternal separation. We would be wise to Stop and meditate on the gravity of this subject.

The Bible tells us that Jesus is the mystery of God, or God's sacred secret. (1 Timothy 3:16) In fact the Bible tells us that in Christ is hidden "all the treasures of wisdom and knowledge". (Colossians 2:2, 3) To understand God's sacred mystery, we need to begin to unravel the Person of Jesus, we need to begin to answer the question; who do *you* say that He is?

I am emphasizing this question because the question is not merely for the Jehovah's Witness; this applies also to you, and for the millions who claim to be "Christians". The whole point is that who we say Jesus Christ is really matters. In fact what we do with Jesus and who we identify him as will determine our eternal fate. So before we as Christians take our finger and wag it in the face of a Jehovah's Witness, a Mormon or a Muslim, we need to be prepared to ask ourselves this very important question of who Christ is. Do we live life as if we know the reality of the Person of Jesus? Are we so convinced of the evidence for Jesus that we are willing to put our life and reputation on the line for his name sake?

JW's take pride in "taking in knowledge" of Jesus and Jehovah, and I was right up there boasting in my acquired knowledge, but knowledge alone could not bring me into a saving relationship with Christ. I took in as much knowledge as I could, thinking that by doing so I would "know" Jesus better. There is a huge, even an eternal difference between "knowing" Jesus, and simply knowing about Jesus. Jesus had some choice words for people like me, he said:

"**Not everyone saying to me, 'Lord, Lord,' will enter into the kingdom of the heavens,** but the one doing the will of my Father who is in the heavens will. Many will say to me in that day, 'Lord, Lord, did we not prophesy in your name, and expel demons in your name, and perform many powerful works in your name?' And yet then I will confess to them: **I never knew YOU! Get away from me, YOU workers of lawlessness."** – Matthew 7:22-23 NWT

Jesus is not interested in how much knowledge you have, he is not impressed with all the things you may even do in his name. Many Christians end up making the same mistake as the Jehovah's Witness, they feel their pursuit of knowledge or apologetics equals a right relationship with God. It doesn't. The question is not how much do you *know*, the question really is, are you *known* by Him. If we were stand before Jesus Christ the Great Judge, will we present to him a laundry list of so-called "knowledge" and think we have eternal life through that? To know Him and to be known by Him is eternal life, something I felt as a Witness was far from my grasp.

We have already examined who Jesus is in the Watchtower, but in reflection I stop and ask myself, who was Jesus to *me* as one of Jehovah's Witnesses?

WHO DID I SAY HE WAS?

As a Jehovah's Witness, Jesus was somewhat a mystery to me, not in the sense that I didn't know anything about him. I knew a lot about Jesus; at least I thought I did. I had memorized Scripture verses about Jesus and his teachings, I could quote him and tell you about all the miracles he did. But Jesus was a mystery to me in the sense that I felt as if a wall existed between Him and I, as though I was looking at him through a broken mirror. Jesus to me was sort of God's sidekick, a prominent figure in the Bible, but it was ultimately all about Jehovah the Father and not about Jesus. I was always aware of Jesus, but he was never the big picture. As I began increasing in knowledge I began to see the role Jesus played in Scripture, that he was Jehovah's beloved Son, his firstborn creation. I could relate to Jesus as a Son, I always wanted to make my parents proud and I saw Jesus as a role model who always did the will of the Father.

I was impressed with Jesus, I aspired to be like him, and I also aspired to reach many like he did. Jesus was never God in my world, but I admired him and later in life began having a sense of reverence for the man who died for me. You see as one of Jehovah's Witnesses, we were taught to have a deep appreciation for the Ransom sacrifice of Jesus Christ. Every year the Watchtower celebrates its only official "holiday", the Memorial of the Lord Jesus Christ. An estimated 17 million people from all over the world attend Kingdom Halls and observe the sacraments of Jesus represented in the wine and the unleavened bread. This day is especially exciting for Witnesses for it is a time that the Witnesses have set apart to honor Jesus Christ.

The teachings I had grown up with concerning the Jesus of the Watchtower made perfect sense to me, Jesus is called "the Son of God" in the Bible, Jesus prayed to the Father, surely then he could not be God. Jesus was always presented as a secondary person next to Jehovah. He didn't seem as important as the Father; Jesus would be mentioned in our meetings but only as an example, never to offer up praise, glory, wisdom and blessing to the Son. (Revelation 5:12) The Jesus "God-man" doctrine of Christendom made little sense to me, nevertheless the Trinity doctrine which in my mind was pagan demonic nonsense. Jesus was never equal to the Father, but always in subjection to his God, Jehovah. This was the only thing that made sense to me, the only thing I could accept. To me Jesus Christ was a figure, not necessarily an intimate person.

In time as I progressed in Bible knowledge I found myself becoming more intrigued and reverent of Jesus, especially when I would read the New Testament. I was beginning to see how essential Jesus was to Jehovah's purpose, and was amazed at his selfless example of love and obedience. Although I did not believe in his full deity, I couldn't help but see Jesus in a more reverent way. As Witnesses we were encouraged to love and admire Jesus, but he was never worthy of our praise, our worship or our prayers. I felt somewhat disconnected from Him. I felt like I had a pretty decent relationship with the Father, I knew a lot about Jehovah! Yet Jesus always felt distant, even in the meetings at the Kingdom Hall we never practiced exalting Jesus Christ.

There were times when I would go to the Kingdom Hall and not have Jesus mentioned the whole entire time until the closing prayer, since every Jehovah's Witness closes their prayers "in the name of Jesus", yet their prayers are never directed to Jesus personally. I once decided to tally down how many times Jesus is referred to in contrast to how many times Jehovah was referred to. The result was something like Christ being mentioned 2 to 4 times in any given meeting, and the rest would be about Jehovah or the preaching ministry or moral living. When Jesus was mentioned it was almost like he was used to only make a point, as if he was just one of the prophets, it was always devoid of his presence and power.

As much as I wanted to have a close relationship with Jesus I constantly felt as if I was running into a wall, a wall of hostility. Jehovah's Witnesses know in their hearts that they in reality have no true relationship with Jesus Christ as they do with Jehovah. They merely take orders from him as they would the prophets; they admire him from afar and claim to appreciate all that he has done through the ransom, yet in their hearts, as there was in mine is, exists a void. Why does that void exist? Because if Jesus is just an Angel then there was no true work of redemption, there is no salvation for an

Angel cannot carry the sins of mankind let alone save it. A Jesus Christ that is a created "god" cannot restore what took the True God to create.

You see the heart of our message as Jehovah's Witnesses was never all about Jesus. The Gospel according to the Watchtower is not to come unto Jesus for salvation, rather the Watchtower says that the witness or gospel given is "the invitation to **come to Jehovah's organization for salvation**" (*The Watchtower*, November 15, 1983). In any system of thought in which Christ is not supreme, something or someone else comes in to hold that place. I was kept from having a relationship with Christ because I was constantly being directed into serving the Organization.

I defined Jesus Christ as the Watchtower allowed me to define him, as a different Jesus then the one we encounter in Scripture, who the real Jesus warned us would be prevalent in the last days. (Matthew 24:5, 11; Galatians 1:6-9) I myself stubbornly held onto the Jesus of the Watchtower, believing that the Watchtower would never lie to me or guide me to a false understanding of Christ.

WHAT CHANGED?

Obviously I am no longer one of Jehovah's Witnesses, and I certainly do not believe in the Jesus of the Watchtower. So what began to change my perception of Jesus Christ you may ask? How did I go from being a devout Jehovah's Witness to confessing Jesus as my Savior? The answer is quiet simple: It was Jesus. Jesus said "Everyone the Father gives Me will come to Me, and the one **who comes to Me I will never cast out**." (John 6:37 HCSB) I began to notice as a JW that I did not have a New Testament relationship with Christ. What do I mean by that? As I began to study the Scriptures I began to notice that the New Testament was in fact all about Jesus Christ, every single page was saturated with the life, teachings, and power of the Lord Jesus Christ. In the meetings at the Kingdom Hall I made it my goal to mention and give due honor to Jesus during my comments or talks at the Hall. The more I studied the more I noticed that not only was the New Testament all about Jesus, but the whole Bible was pointing to the Person of Jesus Christ. After slowly coming to these realizations I desperately wanted "know Him and the power of His resurrection" (Philippians 3:10, HCSB), I was no longer content with the little I was being told about Jesus at the Kingdom Hall, I wanted to know him as the early Christians did where they knew Christ to the point of dying in his name.

The Watchtower had always told me that the only way I could ever attain everlasting life and a right standing before Jesus and Jehovah was to be associated with "the Organization". The organization took and sat In the place of Christ, claiming that it was the *sole* communication between mankind and God. This notion was mesmerizing as a Witness, as I explained in previous chapters I was held captive by this idea regarding the exclusivity of the Watchtower Organization. But it was not until I began to seriously examine the Person of Christ in the New Testament, did I find that this notion of the Society being God's channel, the only way to Paradise, was not only true but was taking the rightful attributes of Jesus Christ and applying it to the Organization of Jehovah's Witnesses.

The truth of Jesus finally began to unravel to me. My whole life began to change as I began to know and have fellowship with the real Jesus, the Jesus that said "Come to Me, all of you who are weary and burdened, and I will give you rest". (Matthew 11:28, HCSB) I began to notice that all this time Christ was actually directing mankind to Himself as the source of rest, life, salvation, blessings, mercy and love. (John 14:6) I began to see that it wasn't about a religion or organization, rather it was all about a Person, Jesus Christ.

As I began to search the Scriptures I kept being confronted more and more with the utter reality of the supremacy of Christ throughout the Story of God. I could remember just being floored with how nearly everything in Scripture is there to point us to Jesus. He is the Big Picture! The average Jehovah's Witness pays lip service to Jesus Christ and seemingly affirms Christ as a key player in their religion, but as a person who lived it from infancy I can tell you that it is a superficial honor. Jesus quoting Isaiah said "This people honors me with their lips, but their heart is far from me." (Matthew 15:8, NWT) I would search through Watchtower literature in search of spiritual fulfillment and words of exaltation of Jesus, yet always coming back empty and hungry for the Word. I grew tired of searching through the pages of the Watchtower for something I wasn't going find; I grew tired of meetings after meetings at the Kingdom Hall with no Jesus. So I took on the challenge set by Jesus himself "Ask, and it will be given to you; seek, and you will find; knock, and it will be opened to you. For everyone who asks receives, and the one who seeks finds, and to the one who knocks it will be opened". (Matthew 7:7-8, NWT) And Jesus proved to be faithful to his words. I knocked, and Jesus answered. If you wish to read my full testimony, you can read it in the last chapter of this book, "My Witness".

As it was with the Jewish people from the time the Law of Moses was given, a veil remained over their eyes down through the centuries, a veil that can only be lifted in Christ. (2 Corinthians 3:13-16) No words can better describe the condition of those following the Watchtower Society then the very words of our Lord Jesus Christ in John 5:39, 40: "You pore over the Scriptures because you think you have eternal life in them, **yet they testify about Me**. And **you are not willing to come to me so that you may have life**."

The Witness becomes so obsessed in their quest to "take in knowledge" that they forget to come to the One in whom is stored all the treasure of wisdom and knowledge, and the only One who can give everlasting life, Jesus Christ. I once was far off from Christ; I was an enemy hostile to the reality of who he really is. I had no real relationship with Jehovah because I did not have the Son. (1 John 2:23) My whole life changed however, the moment I came to know the real Jesus. The next chapter we will learn about who the real Jesus is according to the Scriptures.

CHAPTER 10

JESUS ACCORDING TO THE SCRIPTURES

"**Y**ou are the Christ, the Son of the living God." (Matthew 16:14 NWT) This most basic and simple confession of faith uttered by the Apostle Peter is crucial in unraveling the identity of Jesus Christ. First of all we must understand that there are some obvious undistinguishable differences between the Christ that we speak of and the Christ the JW speaks of. Jehovah's Witnesses and Christians alike both claim to affirm Peter's confession that Jesus is the Son of God. Yet when we examine what the Bible teaches concerning Jesus and what the JW's claim the Bible teaches in regard to Christ, we see two different stories, two different perspectives, two different Jesus's.

When the Jehovah's Witness say Jesus is the Son of God and the Christian affirms that, in reality we mean two very different things. For the JW, Jesus is "called the Son of God because he was created with qualities like those of his Father". (*The Watchtower*, March 1st, 2013 pg. 16) What the Witness really means when he says that Jesus is God's Son is that Jesus is a literally created by God as an Angel.

One cannot afford to merely examine certain aspects of the Bible and pick and choose what they like regarding Christ then disregard the rest. When we examine the Person of Jesus in the Holy Scriptures it is important that we examine the whole of Scripture so that we can see the full picture of Jesus. If we begin to ignore certain verses concerning Christ because it does not agree with our preconceived ideas of Christ, then we break the Scriptures and form a Jesus after our own image. Now that you know about the Watchtower Jesus, let us examine the Scriptures to see who the Real Jesus is and who he is not, for there is no discussion is more paramount.

JESUS- "SON OF MAN & SON OF GOD"

"Are you the Christ the Son of the Blessed One? I am; and YOU persons will see the Son of man sitting at the right hand of power and coming with the clouds of heaven."- Mark 14:61-62 NWT

Jesus is frequently called the "the Son of Man" throughout the Scriptures, 88 times in the New Testament. When confronted by the High Priest he was asked "By the living God I put you under oath to tell us whether you are **the Christ the Son of God!**" Jesus responds "You yourself said [it]. Yet I say toYOUmen, from henceforth **YOU will see the Son of man** sitting at the right hand of power and coming on the clouds of heaven." (Matthew 26:63-64 NWT) Throughout Scripture we are confronted with a Messianic figure that is divine and yet is a 'son of man'. In Daniel 7:13 the Prophet receives a prophetic vision of this Messiah and says "I kept on beholding in the visions of the night, and, see there! **With the clouds of the heavens someone like a son of man** happened to be coming".

Have you ever stopped to think why Jesus is called the Son of Man? The Bible is clear that 'Son of Man', a title that Jesus used more than any other to describe himself, is used to emphasize both his fulfilling Messianic prophecy and to emphasize the reality of the Incarnation; that Jesus was fully man the Word made flesh. In the book of Ezekiel, the prophet Ezekiel is called the "son of man" 93 times; this was done to emphasize Ezekiel as a human being, a man. In Biblical times to be called the "son of" something was to note that they were of the same class or essence. For instance in 1 Kings 20:35 the title "sons of the prophet" meant that they were prophets. In Ephesians 2:2 it talks about the "sons of disobedience" referring to those who are by nature disobedient. So clearly then Jesus is the "Son of Man", truly human in every sense. But is he just a human?

Jesus is also called the Son of God. In the mind of the JW one of the strongest barriers in accepting Jesus as God is the fact that Jesus is called the Son of God. They believe that the statement exempts Christ from being God, but what does the title "Son of God" really means? Christians have always believed that Jesus possesses two natures; he is fully God and fully human. What then does it mean when the Christian affirms that Jesus is God's Son? The Biblical and Historical faith has always understood that to mean that Jesus Christ has a begotten or unique relationship with Father for he shares in the very nature and substance of God. (John 5:19; Hebrews 1:2, 3; Philippians 2:6) Just as I share in the same humanity or substance as my father, so Jesus enjoys an eternal begotten relationship with the Father sharing and existing eternally in his essence. The Jews understood that if he was truly claiming to be the Son of God that he was in effect claiming to be God. It is evident "he was also **calling God his own Father, making himself equal to God**". (John 5:19) The JW will try and point out the following verse and claim that Jesus cannot be God for in it Jesus says "Most truly I say to YOU, The Son cannot do a single thing of his own initiative, but only what he beholds the Father doing. For whatever things that One does, these things the Son also does in like manner". (John 5:20, NWT)

Notice however that Jesus never says he is inferior to the Father, but that he works in sync with the Father, as would be totally expected in the unity of the Trinity. The Son cannot do anything apart from the Father, but realize that He himself said that he can do anything he sees the Father do. Who other than God himself can do in like manner the works of the Father? Jesus also goes a step further to declare his equality with the Father by stating "that **all may honor the Son just as they honor the Father**. He that does not honor the Son does not honor the Father who sent him". (John 5:23 NWT) Jesus could not make himself clearer, He demands and is worthy of the same and equal honor as God the Father.

How then could Jesus say that He did not know the day or the hour of his return but that only the Father knew? (Matthew 24:36) How could he also state that the Father was greater than he was? (John 14:28) As fully man Jesus took on the same human limitations that we have. Jesus experienced pain, hunger, happiness, and sorrow "he emptied himself and took a slave's form and came to be in the likeness of men. More than that, when he found himself in fashion as a man, he humbled himself and became obedient as far as death." (Philippians 2:7-8 NWT) In his self-humiliation Jesus willingly took on human limitations without ever ceasing to be God. As the 'Son of Man' Jesus had a limited finite body (Mark 3:9), but as the 'Son of God' or in his deity he could be everywhere and anywhere (John 1:48; Matthew 18:20; 28:20). As a human being he had limited knowledge, even in regard to his Second Coming (Matthew 24:36), but as God he did in fact "know all things" (John 2:24-25; 6:64; 16:30).

The fact that Jesus in John 14:28 says the Father is greater than him shows that Christ is in submission to the One who sent Him, and that the Father is greater in position, just as husbands are in a greater position in authority relative to their wives. (1 Corinthians 11:3; Ephesians 5:22-23) The Father is greater, but that doesn't make him "better" than the Son, just as husbands are not "better" than their wives ontologically. Jesus even said a few verses before in John 14:12 that his followers would do "greater" works than the ones he himself did while on earth. Does that mean that our works can be better than the works of Jesus? By no means! Greater does not always equal better.

The Scriptures state that "in Christ **all the fullness of the Deity lives in bodily form**" or "all the fullness of God" dwells in the man, Christ Jesus. (Colossians 2:9 NIV, NLT) The New World Translation states that "the fullness of the **divine quality** dwells bodily", translating the Greek word "*Theotēs*" as "divine quality" when in fact it means divinity, deity or God-ship (See Romans 1:20 NWT). But instead of getting hung up on the translation of that word, I rather look to the word we can all agree on the word translated as "fullness" (Greek "Plērōma") which has the meaning of 'completion'. Jesus has the fullness, the completion or the completeness of God's divine nature or quality in "bodily form".

Jesus is one person the God-man, fully man and fully God, Son of Man and Son of God. Those titles are not titles of inferiority as the Witnesses believe, but they are titles denoting Jesus Christ as the Incarnate Word, God manifested in the flesh. (John 1:1-18)

JESUS- "BETTER THAN THE ANGELS"

"So he has become better than the angels, to the extent that he has inherited a name more excellent than theirs." – Hebrews 1:4 NWT

One of the most damnable teachings of Jehovah's Witnesses is their identification of Jesus as Michael the Archangel, the foremost angel in Jehovah's angelic family. Yet the Jesus of the Scriptures is presented not as an angel, but as one much greater. To be sure that Christ is no mere angel let us examine some verses in Hebrews chapter 1 and 2.

Jesus is shown to be far better, more excellent, far superior, and greater than all the angels. The writer of the book of Hebrews is noticeably making an effort to make a point to the reader, that Christ by whom God now speaks and "whom he(God) appointed heir of all things, and through whom he made the systems of things", is not a mere creation let alone an angel. (Hebrews 1:2 NWT) Jesus is indeed shown to be "the Word" by whom God has made himself known to mankind and through whom he also created the universe. The writer of Hebrews goes to lengths to declare the full supremacy of Christ not just over the angels but over the whole of creation as heir or the preeminent one over all things. What comes next defies all logic if one were to believe that Jesus was Michael or any other angel, for the Bible then declares "He is the reflection of [his] glory **and the exact representation of his very being,** and **he sustains all things by the word of his power**". (Hebrews 1:3 NWT) Absolutely incredible! Stop and think for a second, Jesus is the very reflection of Jehovah God himself and the exact imprint or representation of his being, praise God! What an astounding statement, what an unfathomable truth that Jesus is in himself exactly like the Father in every way according to his nature. He is not however merely "like" the Father in character as the Watchtower contends, but according to their translation he is exactly the representation or equal of his nature. So quiet literally all that makes the Father truly Jehovah, what makes him God dwells exactly and equally in Christ. Can any such thing truly ever be said of an angel, no matter how great? Would the Creator who said "I am Yahweh, that is My name; I will not give My glory to another" really make an angel the 'reflection of his glory'? (Isaiah 42:8, HCSB)

But it doesn't stop there; Jesus has yet another role as he "sustains all things by the word of his power". He is not merely a reflection or image of God; he is the very Sustainer of all things. He doesn't sustain a 'few things' or 'all other things' but sustains **all things**. Notice also by which authority or power he does this, "by the word of **his power**". The Witness is here without excuse, they cannot say that Jesus has to rely on Jehovah's power to sustain all things, but the testimony of Scripture is clear, He sustains all things by his powerful word. Colossians 1:16-17 paints yet another picture of Christ as Creator and Sustainer it says "For by him **all things were created,** in heaven and on earth, **visible and invisible, whether thrones or dominions or rulers or authorities**—all things were created through him and **for him.** And he is before all things, and **in him all things hold together.**" (ESV)

Something I would like to direct our attention to isn't just the part in which it says he created all things, because the Witness already has an answer for that for in their Bible the Watchtower has inserted the word "other" so the text will read he created "all other things" even though the Greek word for "other" is nowhere to be found in the Greek text. But I want to focus on where it states that by means of him were created all things "no matter whether they are thrones or lordships or governments or authorities". (NWT) What is of Historical and Theological importance is to note that a heresy or false doctrine began to float around the early church which taught that angels were the means to approach God and served as mediators between God and man. Both Paul in Colossians and the writer in Hebrews wrote to the church regarding this manner in order to combat this false teaching. Some within the Christian Congregation even began giving undue glory to certain angels. When Paul refers to "thrones" and "authorities" he is actually referring to heavenly angelic beings. The Apostle Paul makes no mistake about it, Jesus is Lord, creator and sustainer over all the angels, and that would include Michael the Archangel. This ancient heresy has found its way back in modern times in the teaching of the Jehovah's Witnesses, giving undue glory to an angel and making Michael equal to Christ.

The New Testament book of Hebrews states: "For example, **to which one of the angels did he ever say: "You are my son; I, today, I have become your father**"? And again: "I myself shall become his father, and he himself will become my son"?" (Hebrews 1:5, NWT) This verse is a witness or testimony from God the Father regarding the Son, and he poses a question regarding the uniqueness of Jesus Christ, he asks when has the Father ever begotten and called an angel to be his unique Son? The Jehovah's Witness believes that God cannot tell a lie (Titus 1:2), thus the Witness needs to be confronted with the words of God the Father himself and ask them how Jesus can be Michael the Archangel if Jehovah God has never begotten an angel.

Hebrews 1:6 in the NWT states "But when he again brings his Firstborn into the inhabited earth, he says: "**And let all God's angels do obeisance to him.**"". Now in traditional translations of the Bible it reads as "And let all God's angels worship Him". It is important to point out that the Greek word translated as "obeisance" in the NWT is the same word used in Matthew 4:8 when Jesus tells the Devil that only God must be worshiped. Jesus here in reality is being worshiped by the multitudes of angels by the command of God the Father. But one thing however is clear even in the New World Translation; this act of reverence or worship is being performed by **all** the angels, which would also include Michael the Archangel. Jesus is shown to be far greater than the angels, he is set apart from them, he is Lord over them, he even created them according to Hebrews 1:2, John 1:1-3, and Colossians 1:16. Jesus is far better than the angels.

The Book of Hebrews also makes it clear that the world to come will not be under subjection to any angel; it is written "For it is **not to angels that he has subjected the inhabited earth** to come, about which we are speaking". (Hebrews 2:5, NWT) Jehovah Witnesses believe that Jesus rules as King over God's Kingdom and will rule over mankind in a restored paradise earth, but the Scripture is clear that the earth to come will not be under subjection to an angel. Jesus is the King of kings and Lord of lords; it is to his Kingship and Lordship that the earth and all of creation will be in submission to. (Revelation 19:16)

JESUS- "LORD OF ALL"

"For there is the same Lord over all, who is rich to all those calling upon him."- Romans 10:12 NWT

Jesus is Lord. This statement is the cornerstone of the faith that the Son of God came down from the Heavens he created, "who, **existing in the form of God**, did not consider equality with God as something to be used for His own advantage. Instead **He emptied Himself by assuming the form of a slave**, taking on the likeness of men. And when He had come as a man in His external form, **He humbled Himself by becoming obedient to the point of death**—even to death on a cross. For this reason God highly exalted Him and **gave Him the name that is above every name, so that at the name** of Jesus every knee will bow—of those who are in heaven and on earth and under the earth— **and every tongue should confess that Jesus Christ is Lord, to the glory of God the Father.**"- Philippians 2:5-11 HCSB.

Jesus Christ is "Lord of all" (Acts 10:36; Romans 10:12 NWT). He is Lord over the elements and the storms (Psalm 107:25-30 compare Mark 4:39-40), He is Lord over the Sabbath (Matthew 12:8), He is Lord over the sick and sinners (Marks 2:5-11), He is Lord over the wicked spirits and the Enemy (Luke 10:17-20), He is Lord over David (Matthew 22:41-45), He is Lord over Israel (Acts 2:36), He is Lord over God's Kingdom (Colossians 1:13), He is Lord over the Church which is his bride (Matthew 16:18; Ephesians 5:23-25; Colossians 1:18), He is Lord over Jew and Gentile (Romans 10:11-12), He is Lord over salvation (Romans 10:9-13), He is Lord over every "rule and authority and power and dominion, and above every name that is named, not only in this age but also in the one to come" (Ephesians 1:21 ESV). He is Lord over life (Acts 1:14-15), He is Lord over the living and over the dead, He is Lord over the Judgment to whom we will give an account (Revelation 1:17-18; Romans 14:9-12 compare 2 Corinthians 5:10), He is Lord worthy to "receive power, and riches, and wisdom, and strength, and honor, and glory, and blessing" (Revelation 5:12); He is Lord over the Heavens and the Earth (Colossians 1:16-17), He is Lord over the New Heavens and the New Earth (Matthew 19:28; Revelation 21:1-4, 9-11); He is Lord of lords and King of kings (Revelation 19:16); He is the "Lord of Glory" (1 Corinthians 2:8); He is the Lord our Shepard (Psalms 23:1; John 10:14); He is Lord over believers and unbelievers, He is Lord over me, He is Lord over you, He is Lord over everyone and everything that has ever existed and will exist. If there is something you should know it's that Jesus is LORD! Hallelujah, He is truly "Lord of all".

To know him as Lord is essential to the theme of the Scriptures and the key to understanding Jesus. Growing up in the Witness religion I began noticing more as I got older that Jesus was not being emphasized in our meetings or in our literature. As I mentioned in previous chapters, at the Kingdom Hall Jesus would only be mentioned a handful of times during a meeting if at all. Just as strange was the lack of respect for his title as Lord, for when Jesus was mentioned in the meetings it was mostly to prove a point, like his words and command to preach the Good news. But rarely did I come across Christ exalting language; rarely did I hear Jesus referred to as 'our Lord', for even in the pages of the Watchtower many times Jesus would be referred to as "their Lord" in reference to the Apostles and early disciples.

Because the Watchtower maintains that false religions have conspired to take the name "Jehovah" out of the Bible and Christianity and substitute with the title "Lord", I feel that many Jehovah's Witnesses without even being fully conscious of it have become programed to view the title of 'Lord' with superstition or dislike.

To the Jehovah's Witness the word "Lord" is a title of respect that can mean 'Sir' or 'master', since in Watchtower theology Jesus is an exalted spirit creature he can rightfully rule over some as 'Lord'. But what is the New Testament description of "Lord"? And what does it mean to confess Jesus as Lord?

While it is true that the Greek word for 'Lord'(Gr: kurios) was used as a title of respect in ancient times, the word also had the meaning of having 'complete control' or 'supreme in authority' as the Strong's Concordance points out. To the New Testament writers however, the meaning is unmistakable. For instance in Jude 4 it refers "to our only Owner and Lord, Jesus Christ" (NWT), the Greek word translated in the New World Translation as "Owner" is "despotēs" which can mean 'master', 'husband', 'Lord' or 'absolute ruler'. Jude was not being redundant in using both terms, for in the New Testament "Lord" is a title of divinity. The New Testament writers often equated the Hebrew name of God, YHWH (Yahweh or Jehovah) with the Greek "Kurios" or Lord. An example in Hebrews 1:10, a passage being addressed to the Son says: "You at [the] beginning, O Lord, laid the foundations of the earth itself, and the heavens are [the] works of your hands." (NWT) This verse was quoted from Psalm 102:25-27 and was originally addressed to Jehovah God, yet we have the writer of Hebrews applying it directly to Jesus Christ. The author of Hebrews equates "Lord" with "Jehovah". We also see in other places where the word "Lord" is directly equated with Jehovah in numerous places in the Christians Greek Scriptures, such as in Romans 10:9-13; 14:8-11. To confess "that 'word in your own mouth,' that Jesus is Lord" is to confess Him as the Jehovah that saves. (Romans 10:9-13; Joel 2:32, NWT)

Identifying Jesus as Lord is not merely acknowledging that He has some authority or ruler ship, but rather that He has "all authority" and is above all rule. (Matthew 28:18) The Lord Jesus is **far above every government and authority** and **power** and **lordship** and **every name named**, not only in this system of things, **but also in that to come.**" (Ephesians 1:21, NWT) To confess Jesus as Lord is to confess that he is the Jehovah of our Salvation, that he has the name above every name. He is above all things; he is the exalted Lord of Glory, the Lord of all!

JESUS- "OUR GOD"

In answer Thomas said to him: "My Lord and my God!" – John 20:28 NWT

The Scriptures record the astonishing confession of faith when Thomas is confronted with the Risen Lord of Glory; he answers Jesus and calls Him "**My Lord and my God!**" (John 20:28) Was Thomas confused or possibly over-zealous in his proclamation?

Certainly if Jesus knew that Thomas was in error he would have certainly corrected him as the Apostle John was corrected when he fell down to wor-ship one of the Angels in Revelation 19:10. How does Jesus react to Thomas calling Him Lord and God? "Jesus said to him: "Because you have seen me have you believed? Happy are those who do not see and yet believe." (John 20:29) Blessed! Jesus affirms his statement and does not rebuke him. He blesses those who believe in Him, in his resurrection and in his Lordship and deity. To Thomas there was no mistake, he knew who Christ was.

Jesus Christ is repeatedly called God throughout the entire Bible, even in the New World Translation. When witnessing to a Jehovah's Witness concerning the deity of Christ the magnitude of John 20:28 cannot be over-stated. This verse reveals that one of the earliest confessions of faith in Jesus and his resurrection was also a confession of his deity. I came to a point in my time when my conscience would continually confront me on this verse, and a question kept reciting in my mind and heart; "Is Jesus my Lord?" Of course he is- I would say. "But is he your God?" This is a perfect question to ask the JW, if Jesus is the Lord and God of Thomas, then he is the Lord and God of you and of all Christians.

The deity of Christ is so unmistakable that it is woven into the very fabric of the story of God's redemption. In the Hebrew Scripture there is an antici-pation for the coming Messiah and Isaiah 9:6, 7 prophesies this concerning Jesus:

"For there has been a **child born to us**, there has been a **son given to us**; and the princely rule will come to be upon his shoulder. And **his name will be called** Wonderful Counselor, **Mighty God, Eternal Father**, Prince of Peace. To the abundance of the princely rule and to peace **there will be no end**, upon the throne of David and **upon his kingdom in order to establish it firmly and to sustain it** by means of justice and by means of righteousness, **from now on and to time indefinite**. The very zeal of Jehovah of armies will do this." (NWT)

Now the familiar objection is that Jesus is only a "mighty God" but is not Almighty God. My question to that is this, In Isaiah 10:21 Jehovah is called the "mighty God", how many "mighty God's" then exist? When I was a JW apologist I would also make the argument that Jesus has the right to be called a god or a mighty God because he acts in the place of the Father, he is the "image of God" and thus can take on certain roles as Jehovah's chief agent. The problem with this argument however is that we are likening a created being to an Almighty God who said "**To whom will YOU people liken me or make [me] equal or compare me that we may resemble each other?**" (Isaiah 46.5 NWT) God is saying that nothing can come even close to match His awesome qualities, power, dignity, names and titles; yet Jesus is freely given all of them. This verse is not merely mentioning idols, but any created thing, for God cannot be likened even to the angelic beings in the Heavens.(Isaiah 46:9) Not only is Christ called "Lord" and "God" throughout the Bible, He is also given the attributes that belong rightly to God alone.

Jesus is the Immanuel, literally "God with us". (Matthew 1:23; Isaiah 7:14) Jesus has the authority to forgive sins and sinners, something only God can do. (Mark 2:5-9, 10-11) Jesus calls himself the "Lord of the Sabbath" and claims absolute authority and dominion over it, even though it was Jehovah God who established it and set it apart. (Matthew 12:3-8; Deuteronomy 5:12) Jesus "was existing in God's form" (Greek: morphe- literally means 'the nature of') meaning he shared in the very nature of his Father, yet he humbled himself by becoming a man, taking the form or nature of a slave and dying on our behalf. (Philippians 2:6-8 NWT)

Even I as a Witness however, I would not oppose to call Jesus a god or a divine one, for in JW theology Jesus is a god by virtue of his relationship as the Fathers chief representative. The JW will be quick to say though that God has no beginning, yet Jesus they say has a beginning. Interestingly the Bible calls Jesus "the Word" who was with God in the beginning, who was not created but was already there eternally with the Father. It says that "**All things** came into existence through him, and **apart from him not even one thing came into existence**". (John 1:3, NWT) The original Greek word translated as "All things" is "pas" (Gr: Πᾶς) which is a conclusive all-encompassing word that means "all, any, every, the whole" having the meaning of "thoroughly, whatsoever, whole, whosoever". Jesus then therefore cannot be a creation for literally "all things" or everything and anything in the realm of creation was created through Him, In Him, By Him, and for Him. A lot of Christians try and use John 1:1 to prove that Jesus is God, but they do it the wrong way. The JW is convinced that John 1:1 is to be translated as "the Word was a god" and not as "God". Little you say or do may convince them otherwise, however as I just demonstrated we can use John chapter 1 to prove Christ is eternal God without even bothering to get into the whole 'a god' debate. The point that we can make with the Biblical account is to point to Jesus as the Creator of all things. The Apostle John is making a clear parallel in chapter 1 of his Gospel with Genesis 1 and is linking the creation account and attributing it to the Person of Jesus Christ, and even the JW will admit that Jesus was a "helper" in creation. Yet the Bible makes it clear that Yahweh was alone in creation and that it was His hand, and He alone who created all things. God declares "I, Jehovah, am doing everything, **stretching out the heavens by myself,** laying out the earth. **Who was with me?**" (Isaiah 44:24 NWT) This statement by God cannot co-exist with the JW belief that Jesus was a "master worker" beside the Father helping create the universe for we understand this verse to teach that no created being was involved in the creation process of the cosmos. God is contending in Isaiah that he alone has the power, capacity and sovereignty to create, that Yahweh alone is the Creator of all things. God had no help and was in need of no one to help him, to call Jesus a created being who helped God create is to call God himself a liar when he inquires the rhetorical, "Who was with me?"

The evidence for the deity of Christ in John chapter one does not end there, in fact John 1:14 declares "And **the Word was made flesh, and dwelt among us,** (and **we beheld his glory,** the glory as of the only begotten of the Father,) full of grace and truth." (KJV) The Word became incarnate; the Word took up his residence among us, the Creator clothed with the created. John also says "**No man has seen God** at any time; **the only-begotten god** (Gr: "monogenēs Theos" literally 'the only-unique God') who is in the bosom [position] with the Father is the one **that has explained him**". (John 1:18) Jesus said that "he who has seen me has seen the Father" (John 14:9) and also "I and the Father **are one**". (John 10:30)

The Apostle Paul wrote to Titus that the "blessed hope" was the glorious manifestation of "our Great God and Savior, Christ Jesus" (Titus 2:12, Kingdom Interlinear), while Peter also used similar language when referring to Jesus Christ as "our God and Savior". (2 Peter 1:1) Christ is not only called and declared to be God on many different occasions; he is also worshiped and rendered sacred service too. Jesus is given the same act of devotion that he said was due only to God, for instance in Matthew 4:10 Jesus tells the Devil that it is the Lord one must worship (Gr: proskuneō) and yet in Matthew verses 2:11;

14:33; 15:25; 20:20; 28:9, 17; and also in Luke 24:52 and Hebrews 1:6 the same Greek word "proskuneō" or worship is directly applied to Christ. In fact in the book of Revelation we see all of creation singing praises to Jesus Christ, "**Worthy is the Lamb** that was slain to receive power, and riches, and wisdom, and strength, and honor, and glory, and blessing. **And every creature which is in heaven, and on the earth, and under the earth, and such as are in the sea, and all that are in them,** heard I saying, Blessing, and honor, and glory, and power, *be* unto him that sitteth upon the throne, and unto the Lamb for ever and ever. And the four beasts said, Amen. And the four and twenty elders **fell down and worshipped him** that liveth for ever and ever."- Revelation 5:12-14 KJV

The greatest witness of the identity and deity of our Lord Jesus Christ is the witness given by God the Father. In Hebrews 1 God the Father makes it clear that the Son is not an Angel, but is in fact God. "**But of the Son he** (the Father) **says, "Your throne, O God,** is forever and ever, the scepter of uprightness is the scepter of your kingdom." (Hebrews 1:8, ESV) Are we to believe in God the Father or in men in whom there is no salvation? As a JW I believed that since Jesus always refers to the Father as "God" then that proved Jesus wasn't God, but as we see even God the Father calls the Son God, it is the ultimate witness to the deity of Jesus Christ. It should also be noted that the New World Translation mistranslates Hebrews 1:8 as "God is your throne forever and ever". It doesn't take a Greek New Testament Scholar to look at that and be left scratching your head. In predictable Watchtower fashion they render a theologically tough verse for them like Hebrews 1:8 and translate it in such a way that not only strips Jesus of his deity but often time makes little to no sense what so ever (See Hebrews 1:8 and Romans 9:5 in the Kingdom Interlinear of the Greek Scriptures printed by JW's). It is clear not only through the narrative of the Scriptures but also by the witness of God the Father that Jesus Christ is Almighty God.

If you are a Christian I hope that this chapter has affirmed your conviction in the Person and deity of Jesus Christ our Lord, or if you are reading this and do not believe that Jesus is the God he claimed to be, I ask you to examine the Jesus of the Bible and the Jesus in the pages of this book and ask yourself, "Is Jesus the Lord of me, and the God of me?" It is my prayer that Jesus would be both your Lord and your God! "No, but go on growing in the undeserved kindness and knowledge of our Lord and Savior Jesus Christ. **To him be the glory both now and to the day of eternity.**"- 2 Peter 3:18 NWT

CHAPTER 11

MAKING SENSE OF THE TRINITY

The Trinity is at the core of the Christian faith and the climax of the revelation of God. It is a doctrine that has been challenged, hated and misunderstood by millions of people and religions throughout the centuries, yet it is a teaching that is at the heart of God's revelation to man. Unfortunately Christians have not done a very good job at defending or clearly teaching this sacred truth, thus opening the door to alternative and erroneous views concerning the nature of God to creep into the Church and the culture.

To the Watchtower and its followers, the idea of a Trinity is anathema. As a Jehovah's Witness I especially despised the teaching of the Trinity, I felt it was a disastrous misrepresentation of Jehovah God and his Son Jesus Christ. Of all of Christendom's teachings, none is more despised by the Witnesses, for they are taught from day one that the Trinity doctrine held by most Christian Churches is a pagan creed and is an abomination and insult in the eyes of the Creator God, Jehovah. The Watchtower Society has written that "to worship God on his own terms means **to reject the Trinity doctrine**... It contradicts what God says about himself in his own inspired Word." (*Should You Believe in the Trinity?*)

The Trinity made little sense to me as a Jehovah's Witness, I looked upon even the notion of the Trinity as a filthy pagan invention adopted by the apostate Catholic Church and later maintained by the Protestants. For me it was simple, Jehovah alone is God and he is our Father. Jesus is God's Son, which means that God created Jesus before anything, and that the Holy Spirit was just an active force, like electricity. This was a lot easier to grasp as a child then the Trinity. When I first heard about the Trinity growing up, I was taken aback by the whole notion, I thought to myself, "How can people believe in such a thing?" I can recall asking my mother about it and affirmed the complete absurdity of the doctrine of the Trinity to me. It was around this time that I was exploring internet blog sites and began "preaching" to people through the internet, I also began to encounter more and more people who believed in the Trinity which in turn motivated me to research the Trinity for myself. The more I learned about it, the more I actually became convinced of my own beliefs. I felt that my religion was the true religion because we took a stand against the doctrine of the Trinity, advocating instead that Jesus and Jehovah are distinct beings with Jesus being a created creature. Not believing in the Trinity made us unique as Jehovah's "Christian" Witnesses. So it begs the question; why do I now believe in the Trinity?

Long story short, what I despised and attacked all my years as a Jehovah's Witness was not actually the Historic and Biblical doctrine of the Trinity. How so? In my mind I always thought when Trinitarians called Jesus God or Jehovah, that they were saying that Jesus is the same Person as God the Father. I would immediately protest saying Jesus prayed and even offered worship to the Father, so how can Jesus be the same person as his Father? When I actually began understanding what Christians meant by the Trinity, it began to make more sense to me. I had confused Modalism with the Trinity. Almost every JW you will encounter has a false understanding of the Trinity. But what ultimately convinced me of the reality of God in Trinity was the Bible itself. This whole chapter will be dedicated to unraveling and making sense of the Trinity for us and helping the Witness understand the mystery of God in Trinity.

Unfortunately many Christians do not have a firm understanding on the doctrine of the nature of God, giving the Jehovah's Witnesses and other Unitarians reason to label the Trinity as "false" and unscriptural. JW's feel vindicated when they question most Christians and they cannot give an ample defense of the Trinity. When a JW and a Christian talk about the Trinity, the JW has a totally different definition of the Trinity then that of orthodox

Christianity. This is why it is important that as Christian we define the Trinity as it has been revealed to us in the Scriptures.

We won't be able to convince the Witnesses of the nature of God if we ourselves are ignorant of its basis and reality in the Scriptures. Our understanding of God's nature is of eternal value, and this is a subject we cannot afford to be wrong on. In this chapter I will endeavor to share the truth of God's Word that brought me into a saving knowledge of God in Trinity, so that in turn we may teach and refute those who contradict it. It is impossible to cover this topic in just one chapter, but by God's grace I will leave behind an outline of Biblical reasons why this former JW now believes in the Trinity.

GOD IN TRINITY

If you were to ask a Jehovah's Witness to define the Trinity, you will likely hear them explain to you that the Trinity is "three gods in one god" or that "the Father, Son and Holy Spirit are all the same person". I have had numerous JW's describe to me the Trinity in these terms. You see, the JW's usually do not even understand what the Christian Trinity is. Before I explain what the doctrine of the Trinity is, let me first tell you what it is not. The Trinity is not Tritheism, the notion that there are three separate God's who may be "one in purpose" such as in the Mormon belief. Neither is it Modalism, the idea that there is One God who has three modes or roles. These teachings have been long denounced and are not reflective of the Biblical definition of the Triune nature of God. One of the reasons why JW's object to the Trinity is because the word "Trinity" is not found in the Bible, but we certainly can find the teaching throughout the revelation of God's Word. Just as the Watchtower Society uses words that are not in the Bible to describe Biblical principle, such as "Theocratic", "Paradise Earth" and "Kingdom Halls", so the Historic Christian faith has used the word Trinity to describe God's eternal nature. The word 'Trinity' comes from a Latin word which means "threefold" or "Three in One". So then it is important then that we establish to the Witness what the Trinity is, and what it is not.

Things to establish:

We believe God is one. Simply put, the Bible reveals to us that there is One eternal self-existing God, Yahweh or Jehovah, (Exodus 3:14-15) and this God is "one Jehovah". (Deuteronomy 6:4)

God is complex and not limited to his nature. God is One in his nature yet we see the divine name and attributes of the "one Jehovah" equally shared between the Person of the Father, (Isaiah 64:8) the Son (Jeremiah 23:5-6; Romans 10:9-13; Hebrews 1:10) and the Holy Spirit. (Acts 5:3-4; Hebrews 3:7-11)

Distinct yet One. Three distinct Persons who the Scriptures call 'Jehovah God' all share in the one nature or essence of God. Though distinct in Person and function, they are one and share in the one "name". (Matthew 28:19)

It is important to establish also that the no Trinitarian would assert that God the Father is the same Person as the Son or the Holy Spirit, rather we recognize that God's one true nature or essence is eternally shared in three Persons, the one Jehovah. The Father is obviously not the Son for he sends the Son, and Jesus is not the Father for he prays to the Father and submits to Him, just as the Holy Spirit is sent by the Father and the Son to testify about Jesus. There is distinction in person not in nature or essence. The Witness will quickly jump in and say "But this is not logical! Therefore it must not be true!" Who says this is not logical? Man? We can barely put our minds around the fact that God is eternal, always existing outside time and matter! God is infinitely complex in his being, yet he makes himself known through the revelation of the Trinity and ultimately and fully in the Incarnation of Jesus Christ. God has made himself known through his Word, Jesus Christ, and has given us the ability to be in communion with Him by his Holy Spirit. The Jehovah's Witness believes that the Trinity defies all logic, but what we need to establish is that regardless to what we uphold as "logic", what matters to us is if the Bible actually teaches that there are three Persons who are Jehovah in name, essence and nature.

As I read the Scriptures and reflect on the nature of God, I come across a God who is revealing himself through his Spoken Word and his Spirit. A person's word or spirit is indistinguishable from the person who possesses it. (1 Corinthians 2:11) Jesus is revealed as the Word who was from the beginning, who existed alongside God and was as to his nature God also. (John 1:1; Genesis 1:26) The Holy Spirit of God also speaks the very words of God, teachings, comforting, exhorting, praying and interceding. (Acts 13:2, 28:25; John 14:26; Romans 8:26-27) God the Father is the head and source of the Godhead; he is the One from whom the Word and the Spirit proceed out of. (1 Corinthians 11:3, 15:24-28) The submission of Christ and the Holy Spirit to the Father in no way diminishes their deity or personhood; it actually shows that order exist in the divine Majesty of the Trinity. We see a similar arrangement in marriage, God says that a woman ought to lovingly submit to her husband as head, not because she is inferior, but because there is order and respect for headship. (1 Corinthians 11:3) Yet it says when the man and woman enter into marriage covenant they are "one flesh". (Genesis 2:24) The Bible says that God is love, yet if God is not Triune in his nature then God cannot be love, for love is a covenant between persons. (1 John 4:8) Whom did God love before the creation? If you're a Jehovah's Witness you believe that Jehovah was all alone before creating Jesus, thus God could not have been love in eternity past for there was no one or nothing to love! But the Bible reveals God has always been in perfect fellowship and relationship within Himself. (Genesis 1:26; John 1:1) God is self-existing, he doesn't need us nor does his attribute of love depend on created things. An earthly example to help us describe the Trinity is Time itself, for time is past, present and future, yet the past is not the present and the present is not the future. All distinct aspects of time, yet it's not three "times" but only one Time. Likewise we see Jesus tell his disciples to "go and make disciples of all nations, baptizing them in the **name** of the Father and of the Son and of the Holy Spirit". (Matthew 28:19, NIV) God's one name is shared by three divine Persons.

As a Jehovah's Witness I would protest, "But where in the Bible is there even a hint of the Trinity? The word Trinity is not even in the Bible!" Yet throughout the Scriptures we see glimpses, and sometimes more than just hints of the revelation of the Trinity. For instance we see it in the title God uses for himself, "Elohim", which is a plural form of the title God, or "El". Through the title 'Elohim' we see the plurality and oneness of the One God. The title Elohim appears 2,570 times, beginning in Genesis 1:1 and later on in that chapter where we see Elohim declare "Let *Us* make man in *our* image, in *our* likeness", and thus "**God** (Elohim) proceeded to create the man in **his** image, in **God's** image **he** created him". (Genesis 1:26, 27, NWT) Point the Witness to verse 26 where we see God use the plural term "us" and "our", and then in verse 27 it says that "he" created man in the singular image. The JW will say that the "us" in Genesis 1:26 is Jehovah using Jesus to create the first human couple, yet the problem is that it says "God proceeded to create the man in his image", thus Jesus according to their own words must be God. We see the plurality of Jehovah in other instances such as in Genesis 19:24 which states, "Then **Jehovah** made it rain sulphur and fire **from Jehovah**, from the heavens, upon Sodom and upon Gomorrah." (NWT) In this verse we literally have two distinct Jehovah's, where Jehovah God initiates it to rain destruction from Jehovah in the Heavens. There is no way of making sense of this verse outside a Trinitarian context. In Amos 4:10-11 we see another one of these statements, this time by the mouth of Yahweh himself: "'I sent a plague among you after the manner of Egypt; I slew your young men by the sword along with your captured horses, and I made the stench of your camp rise up in your nostrils; yet you have not returned to Me,' declares the LORD (Jehovah). 'I overthrew you as **God** overthrew Sodom and Gomorrah". (NASB) Jehovah God speaking says that he overthrew Israel just as "God overthrew Sodom and Gomorrah". We see diversity, complexity, plurality and unity in the nature of the True God, Jehovah. The Scriptures also teach that no man has ever seen God and lived, (Exodus 33:20) yet there are many instances in the Bible where Jehovah God appeared visibly and physically to men, which are referred to as Theophany's. (Genesis 17:1, 18:1; Exodus 24:9-11) The Witnesses often stress the verses in which it says no man has ever seen God, for the Society teaches that Jehovah is an invisible spirit, and no one can or ever will see him. Yet the Witness will have a hard time explaining away Biblical verses such as in Exodus 33:11, which says that "**Jehovah spoke** to Moses **face to face**, just as a man would speak to his fellow", (NWT) and Isaiah 6:1 when Isaiah "got to **see Jehovah**, sitting on a throne lofty and lifted up". (NWT) How can we harmonize the fact that the Bible on one hand as the JW's also say, no one has ever seen God, yet on the other hand it says that Jehovah God was seen? John 1:18 explains, "No one has seen God at any time; the **only begotten God** who is in the bosom of the Father, **He has explained Him**." (NASB) No one has ever seen God the Father, but the only begotten God, Jesus Christ is the one who has made the Father manifest. Jesus is the Jehovah who was seen in the Old Testament Theophany's, and the one who unfolds the mystery of the Trinity.

JESUS AS JEHOVAH GOD

The very words "Jesus is Jehovah" makes the average JW cringe and immediately nod their heads in disapproval. In JW theology the notion is downright wrong and demon inspired. You see when a JW hears a Christian assert that Jesus Christ is Jehovah God, in their minds they think that you are equating Jesus as the same person as the Father. The Watchtower maintains the Unitarian view that only the Father is Jehovah, thus when Trinitarians call Jesus Jehovah the JW thinks you must be referring to Jesus as God the Father. This however is not an accurate description of what Christians believe regarding Christ, for we do not believe that when we say "Jesus is Jehovah" that we are saying that he is the Father, for in the Biblical understanding of the Trinity Jesus is distinct from the Father. As JW's rightly point out Jesus prayed to the Father, glorified the Father, and even worshiped the Father, thus Jesus is clearly seen to be a distinct person from his God and Father. But does this mean that Jesus cannot be God or Jehovah? In the previous chapter I outlined various Scriptures that refer to Jesus as our God, so in this brief section I will outline specific verses that refer to Jesus as Yahweh.

The Bible clearly tells us that there is One God, Jehovah or Yahweh. In Deuteronomy 6:4 it says "Jehovah our God is one Jehovah". Christians in no way deny Mosaic Monotheism, we do however recognize that Jesus is not only given the name "Jehovah" but is shown to also have the qualities that belong to Jehovah God alone. In the previous chapter we identified Jesus as Lord and God, but is he identified with the name and attributes of YHWH (Jehovah)? We can actually show the JW in their New World Translation of the Bible that Jesus is in fact identified not just as "God" but as Jehovah God. The Prophet Jeremiah prophesied concerning the promised Messiah, "There are days coming," is the utterance of Jehovah, "and I will raise up to David a **righteous sprout**. And a **king** will certainly reign and act with discretion and execute justice and righteousness in the land. In his days Judah will be saved, and Israel itself will reside in security. And this is **his name** with which he will be called, **Jehovah Is Our Righteousness**." (Jeremiah 23:5-6, NWT) The King who descends from David's lineage has a name; it is "Jehovah Tsidkenu (our righteousness)", and Jesus is directly given and attributed this name. In Zechariah 11:13 we see an even clearer prophetic picture of who Messiah truly is, for it says "At that, Jehovah said to me: "Throw it to the treasury—the **majestic value** with which **I have been valued** from their standpoint." Accordingly I took the **thirty pieces of silver** and threw it into the treasury at the house of Jehovah." (NWT) Jesus is the fulfillment of this prophecy, being betrayed for 30 pieces of silver even though Jehovah God said that it was the price that **He** was priced at. (Matthew 26:15) In Zechariah 12:10 Jehovah speaking says, "I will pour out on the house of David and on the inhabitants of Jerusalem, the Spirit of grace and of supplication, so that they will look on **Me whom they have pierced**; and they will mourn for Him, as one mourns for an **only son**, and they will weep bitterly over Him like the bitter weeping over a **firstborn**." (NASB)

These verses are significant, for Jehovah identifies himself as the one who will be pierced and the one who would be betrayed. As I began to seriously study the person of Christ and messianic prophecy in the Old Testament, I was amazed at the direct parallels between Jehovah God and the coming Messiah. Zechariah foretells the betrayal, death, resurrection, and return of Jesus Christ. Of his return it says, "**Jehovah** will certainly go forth and war against those nations... And **his feet will actually stand** in that day upon **the mountain of the olive trees**, which is in front of Jerusalem, on the east; and the mountain of the olive trees must be split at its middle, from the sun-rising and to the west... And **Jehovah** my God will **certainly come, all the holy ones** being with him." (Zechariah 14:3-5, NWT) Jesus is the Jehovah who will return at the end of the age with all his saints, and stand upon the Mount of Olives in glory and victory. (1 Thessalonians 3:13; Revelation 1:7)

There are many verses in the New Testament that apply verses that originally applied to Yahweh to Jesus. For instance Psalm 68:18 says, "You have ascended on high; You have carried away captives; You have taken gifts in the form of men, Yes, even the stubborn ones, to reside [among them], O **Jah God**", (NWT) and yet Ephesians 4:7-10 Paul directly says this verse was about Jesus, and that he "fills all things". Romans chapter 10 says that we must confess "Jesus is Lord", to believe that God raised him from the dead, and that all who call upon him will not be put to shame for he is "the same **Lord over all**, who is rich to **all** those **calling upon him**. For "everyone who calls on the **name of Jehovah** will be saved." (Romans 10:9-13, NWT) Verse 13 is a quotation from Joel 2:32 and Paul uses this verse and applies it to Jesus as the Jehovah who saves. We must show the Witness that by its context this verse is explicitly referring to Jesus as Yahweh, for Jesus is the only name under heaven that has the power and authority to save unto the salvation of the believer. (Acts 4:12) Hebrews 1:10-12 is another example of the New Testament linking Jesus as YHWH. In it the writer quotes and uses Psalm 102:25-27 which originally refers to Jehovah as the one who "laid the foundations of the earth itself, and the heavens are [the] works of your hands" and says this Jehovah or Lord is Jesus Christ. It says of Jesus, "They themselves will perish, but you yourself are to **remain continually**; and just like an outer garment they will all grow old, and you will wrap them up just as a cloak, as an outer garment; and they will be changed, but **you are the same**, and your **years will never run out**." (Hebrews 1:10-12, NWT) Jesus is not simply given the divine name of God, he also has the attributes of Jehovah, he is the Creator, Sustainer, Eternal, and Never changing.

The Bible could not be clearer, Jesus **is** Jehovah God. Jesus is the same Jehovah who is Lord, the one "every knee will bend down, every tongue will swear" too. (Isaiah 45:23 NWT; Philippians 2:11; Romans 14:9-11) Jesus is the Jehovah that Isaiah saw with his eyes, high and exalted, and the one John identified as Jesus. (Isaiah 6:1-10; John 12:40-41) Jesus is the same Jehovah who is "the first and the last", the Alpha and Omega. (Isaiah 44:6; Revelation 1:7-18) Jesus is the Jehovah who "examines the minds and hearts" of people. (Jeremiah 17:10; Revelation 2:23) Jesus is the same Jehovah who had the way prepared for him by John the Baptist. (Isaiah 40:3; Mark 1:3) Jesus is the same Jehovah, the good Shepard. (Psalm 23:1; John 10:11) The Jehovah's Witnesses must come to know Jesus as their Jehovah, the Great I Am. (Exodus 3:14; John 8:24, 58) Jesus is the chief agent or representative of the Triune Godhead, (Colossians 1:15; 2:9) he is the incarnate one who manifests the will of the Father, (John 6:38) and the one in whose name the Holy Spirit is sent. (John 14:26) Jesus' role in the Godhead is instrumental to our understanding of God and our eternal salvation.

THE HOLY SPIRIT IS GOD

The Holy Spirit is often overlooked by both Christians and Jehovah's Witnesses, many times we get so apologetic in our defense of the deity of Christ that we forget how essential it is to recognize the person and work of the Holy Spirit, the third member of the Trinity. The Watchtower teaches that the Holy Spirit is neither God nor a person, but is "God's active force". *The Watchtower* of Oct. 1st, 2009 states: "The Scriptures make clear that the **holy spirit is a force** that God uses to accomplish his will... There is a close connection between the holy spirit and the power of God. The holy spirit is the means by which Jehovah exerts his power. Put simply, the holy spirit is **God's applied power**, or his **active force**." Witnesses are taught to view the Holy Spirit as an impersonal 'force' that has no thoughts, will, desire, or personality. In their publications and Bible they do not even capitalize the name Holy Spirit, adding more to their assault on the personhood and deity of the Holy Spirit. I viewed the Holy Spirit as some form of electricity, God's power- but he certainly wasn't a person. Some of the arguments I used and many JW's use today against the Holy Spirit's personhood was to point to Acts 2:1-4 where it says that the believers were "filled with the Holy Spirit", so, the argument goes, how can you be filled with another person if indeed the Holy Spirit is a person? Although they overlook the fact that as believers, Christ is "in us" and we are filled by Jesus, yet they would never deny Christ is a person. (2 Corinthians 13:5; Ephesians 2:10) Are the JW's right however, is the Holy Spirit an active force?

First, it is important that we establish that the Holy Spirit is most definitely a person. Ask the Jehovah's Witness, Can an "active force" speak, have a will and be sinned against? Acts 13:2 in the NWT reads, "As they were publicly ministering to Jehovah and fasting, the **holy spirit said**: "Of all persons set Barnabas and Saul apart for **me** for the work to which **I have called them**." Electricity, power and an active force do not have the ability to speak; only persons with minds can speak. The Spirit clearly has a mind, "And he who searches our hearts knows the **mind of the Spirit**, because the Spirit **intercedes** for God's people in accordance with the will of God." (Romans 8:27, NIV) The Holy Spirit has a will, "But one and the same **Spirit** is active in all these, distributing (gifts) to each person as **He wills**." (1 Corinthians 12:11, HCSB) The Holy Spirit speaks, has will, calls and sets apart people, and also intercedes for God's people, all traits that are incompatible with the Watchtowers teaching on the Holy Spirit. Jesus while preparing his disciples with the reality that he was leaving them to be with the Father, that he would send them "another Counselor (helper, comforter) to be with you forever. He is the Spirit of Truth." (John 14:16-17, HCSB) The Holy Spirit is a counselor, a comforter, asked with JW if they have ever been comforted with electricity or some other "active force". Also, point them to Jesus' words later in that chapter, "But the **Counselor**, the **Holy Spirit**--the Father will send Him in My name--will **teach** you all things and **remind** you of everything I have told you." (John 14:26, HCSB) Clearly no impersonal force can comfort, teach and remind. The Bible also says that one can sin against the Spirit, (Matthew 12:31) obviously one cannot sin against impersonal forces. Once you demonstrate to the Witness that the Holy Spirit is a person, we need to demonstrate the purpose and ministry of the Holy Spirit. The primary ministry of the Holy Spirit is to convict mankind of sin, and glorify the Lord Jesus Christ. We see this in Jesus' own statement in John 16:13-14; "when that one arrives, the spirit of the truth, **he** will guide YOU into all the truth, for **he** will not speak of his own impulse, but what things **he hears** he will **speak**, and he will declare to YOU the things coming. That one will **glorify me**". (NWT) The Holy Spirit leads us into the truth of Jesus, convicts us of our sins, and glorifies Jesus. The Spirit of God also prays for us in our weakness, for "In the same way the Spirit also joins to help in our weakness, because we do not know what to pray for as we should, but the Spirit Himself intercedes for us with unspoken groaning's." (Romans 8:26, HCSB) The Witness needs to come to the reality that the Spirit of Truth is no mere active force, but a person who loves them and wants to intercede for them, instruct them and lead them to Jesus for all the truth. Now that we can demonstrate that the Holy Spirit is a person, can we also prove by Scripture that the Holy Spirit is also Jehovah God?

The Bible teaches that the Holy Spirit is God, in Acts 5:3-4 "Peter said, "Ananias, why has Satan filled your heart to **lie** to the **Holy Spirit** and keep back part of the proceeds from the field? ... You have not **lied** to men **but to God!**" (HCSB) Peter calls the Holy Spirit God, for he said Ananias lied to the Holy Spirit and that he had not lied to men but to God. The Bible also gives the Holy Spirit the attributes of God, such as the fact that the Holy Spirit is eternal, Hebrews 9:14 says "how much more shall the blood of Christ, who through the **eternal Spirit** offered himself without blemish unto God". (ASV) The Bible also teaches that the Spirit of God is omni-present, omniscient, and omnipotent. (Psalm 139:7-10; 1 Corinthians 2:10; Luke 1:35) The Holy Spirit authors the inspiration of the Scriptures, (2 Peter 1:20-21) and interprets Scripture. (1 Corinthians 2:14) And something that is vital to share with the Witness in their own Bible is the fact that the Holy Spirit is the Lord Jehovah. 2 Corinthians 3:17-18 says in the New World Translation, "Now **Jehovah is the Spirit**; and where the **spirit of Jehovah** is, there is freedom. And all of us, while we with unveiled faces reflect like mirrors the glory of Jehovah, are transformed into the same image from glory to glory, exactly as done by **Jehovah the Spirit**." This is a clear declaration of the divinity and identity of the Holy Spirit. In Hebrews 3:7-11 we have an Old Testament quotation, Psalm 95:7-11 that was originally spoken by Jehovah God, being attributed to the Holy Spirit. "Therefore, as the **Holy Spirit says**: Today, if you hear His voice, do not harden your hearts as in the rebellion on the day of testing in the wilderness, where your fathers **tested me, tried me**, and saw **my works** 10 for 40 years. Therefore I was provoked with that generation and said, "They always go astray in their hearts, and they have not known my ways." So I swore in my anger, "They will not enter my rest." (HCSB) We have the same situation in Acts 28:25-27 and Hebrews 10:15-17 where the Holy Spirit is attributed to speaking the words that Jehovah had originally spoken. (Compare Isaiah 6:9-10) The Holy Spirit is Yahweh, Jehovah the Spirit.

"GOD WILL BE ALL IN ALL"

As you lead a Jehovah's Witness through these verses, pray that the Holy Spirit will actually convict them of the awesome reality of the person, work and deity of each member of the Trinity. We need also keep in mind that we are in tune with the gifts of the Spirit as we give them a Witness concerning this Bible truth (Galatians 5:22-26) Presenting these important Bible verses concerning the Trinity is meant to move the Witness to the True and everlasting Triune God, Yahweh. Only the Holy Spirit can lead a JW to a scriptural understanding of God's nature, for these are matters that are spiritually discerned. (1 Corinthians 2:14) My honest advice in regard to witnessing to the Jehovah's Witness about the Trinity is to not get in long winded debates regarding it. The Witnesses love attacking the doctrine of the Trinity; once they find out that you believe it they will ambush you with Bible verses and arguments against it. It is easy to get frustrated and confused in an already confusing topic when speaking to JW's. If the Witness continues to bring up the Trinity, give them a verse or two for them to think about, ask them to pray and study those verses and to get back to you. This will force the Witness to examine what the Bible teaches regarding God's nature, and give room for the Holy Spirit to move.

Let us not take for granted the awesome and mysterious God who has revealed himself to us in the Father, the Son and the Holy Spirit. "Now there are different gifts, but the **same Spirit**. There are different ministries, but the **same Lord**. And there are different activities, but the **same God**". (1 Corinthians 12:4-6) We affirm and worship the God and Father of our Lord Jesus Christ, the head and source of the Godhead, by whom all things are. (1 Corinthians 8:6) We affirm and worship Jesus Christ, "our great God and Savior", the Word and revealer of the Father who was eternally with God and was God. (Titus 2:13; John 1:1-18) We affirm and worship the Holy Spirit, who is the eternal Jehovah the Spirit, the Spirit of Christ and the deposit of our salvation. (2 Corinthians 3:17; Hebrews 9:14; Ephesians 1:14) The Godhead is essential in the true worship and salvation of God's people, for we have been "chosen according to the foreknowledge of **God the Father** and set apart by **the Spirit** for obedience and for sprinkling with the blood of **Jesus Christ**." (1 Peter 1:1-2, HCSB) We also believe and affirm that at the end of the ages, when Christ Jesus has defeated the last enemy death, that our Lord Jesus Christ will again come under the full submission of God the Father, and "the Son Himself will also be subject to the One who subjected everything to

Him, so that **God** may be *all in all*", and "Jehovah must become king over all the earth. In that day **Jehovah** will **prove to be one**, and **his name one**". (1 Corinthians 15:28; Zechariah 14:9) This promise in no way denies the divine Trinity, it strengthens it. There is, nor ever will be any division in the Godhead of Jehovah, for no Person in the Godhead ever competes against the other, rather the Father will forever glorify the Son, and the Son will forever glorify the Father, and the Holy Spirit will forever glorify the Son. (John 8:54; 16:14; 17:1-5)

The topic of the Trinity is a topic that every Christian should care deeply about and should be involved in, carefully studying and examining the Scriptures. It's ok to wrestle with God over this deep and complex topic. The debate on the nature of God has gone on for centuries, and this book will certainly not settle it. But we can be assured that at the end, "God will be all in all".

"May the grace of the **Lord Jesus Christ**, and the **love of God**, and the fellowship of the **Holy Spirit** be with you all."- 2 Corinthians 13:14, NIV

CHAPTER 12

DEATH, HEAVEN
AND PARADISE

I t is one of the most daunting questions that we face as human beings, what exactly happens to us when we die? Death is the ultimate statistic, 10 out of 10 people who live will die. Man in his efforts to rationalize death and soften its sting has established rituals and religions to comfort the masses. Most religious people believe in some type of life after death, that a part of a person continues to exist in some form after they have experienced death. The Jehovah's Witnesses however are unique in regard to their belief about what happens to us when we die, in fact the Witnesses tend to sound more atheistic in their belief in death compared to other faiths, for they believe that once you die... well that's it, you no longer exist. The Watchtower reasons: "It's clear teaching is this: *When a person dies, he ceases to exist.* Death is the opposite of life. The dead do not see or hear or think. Not even one part of us survives the death of the body. **We do not possess an immortal soul or spirit.**" (*What Does the Bible Really Teach?* italics theirs)

No immortal soul, no Hell, no conscious afterlife. The Witness will take you to Ecceleciates 9:5, 10 which they believe proves that the dead are unconscious, and they also believe as Genesis 2:7 states, that human beings do not possesses a soul, rather they are souls. Jehovah's Witnesses do not believe that the wicked depart into hellfire or the righteous into Heaven. So what hope does the Witness hope to have? The Witness believes that the Bible teaches that there will be a resurrection of righteous Jehovah's Witnesses and Jewish prophets who will live forever on a paradise earth, while wicked mankind experience no resurrection and remain dead out of existence forever. They also believe that a small number of 144,000 anointed Jehovah Witnesses will rule with Christ in Heaven as resurrected spirit creatures. This is a very deep aspect of Watchtower theology, and I feel as if it is a strong point in JW evangelism. The JW will show the average Christians Bible verses that will send their brains into a nose dive. The average Christian have never read or given much thought to Bible verses that JW's have masterly crafted to fit their theology. As with many of the topics and subjects of this book, this lengthy topic of the afterlife and subsequence hope in Jehovah Witness theology merits a few chapters if not its own book because of the sheer volume of Bible verses, arguments and mindsets that people on the JW and Christian perspective have. Because of limited time and resource, I want to highlight how you can show the JW at your door, how death isn't the end, Heaven can be theirs, and Paradise is greater than they ever imagined!

Growing up in the Witnesses I always felt very confident that our teaching concerning the state of the dead, and the hope of a paradise earth was a clear Bible teaching, it was a belief I had absolute confidence in. I knew without doubt that if I died I would cease to exist but be in Jehovah God's memory, hopefully awaiting a resurrection to a restored paradise earth. We felt that this teaching brought comfort to the people we preached to, they didn't have to worry about eternity in some Hell, or that they would have some vague existence somewhere in the clouds. I felt that we were offering them a real hope, a hope to see dead loved ones restored to a perfect world where war and pain was no more. I believed that we were liberating people from false religious superstition into the light of Bible truth.

Are the Witnesses correct, and there really is no conscious existence after death? Is Hell not as hot as we may have thought? And who really gets to reign with Jesus in Heaven? Let us explore one of the most profound and thought provoking question that mankind has ever asked, what *really* happens to us when we die.

WHAT HAPPENS WHEN WE DIE?

The Jehovah's Witnesses love talking about the state of the dead, and they love going into Old Testament Scriptures which refer to the realm of the dead, the place where every deceased person goes upon death; Sheol which they believe is simply the common grave of mankind ("Hades" is its Greek equivalent). Was Sheol a place of nonexistence, like the Jehovah's Witnesses insist? No. At this point it is important that we establish that Sheol was indeed the realm of the dead in Old Testament times, but that it was not a place of inactivity. In Genesis 37:33-35 Jacob comes across his son Joseph's garment and believes him to be dead, being devoured by an animal, he then goes on to say "I will go down to Sheol to my son, mourning". Clearly Jacob believed he was going to be reuniting with his son in Sheol, he cannot mean simply a "grave" here since he believes Joseph has been devoured by a beast. In Isaiah 14 we see a picture of the disgraced king of Babylon being tossed down into Sheol, where departed spirits greet and mock him (verses 9-11). This too cannot refer to a simple common grave for in verse 18-19 state that this ruler was without a "grave", thus refuting the concept that Sheol always equals the grave rather than a literal place of existence. In the Old Testament Sheol is the opposite of Heaven. (Psalm 139:8) Ezekiel 31:14-18 make mention of Sheol as the place of the underworld, where slain spirits are kept in prison, and where great warriors speak and recount their former glory. (Ezekiel 32:21) Sheol was essentially the waiting place of the dead, before Christ resurrection and ascension all mankind, both righteous and wicked went down into Sheol. Jesus talking about Hades, the Greek equivalent to Sheol, said in the parable of the rich man and Lazarus that in Hades or Sheol existed "a great chasm has been fixed between us and YOUpeople, so that those wanting to go over from here to YOUpeople cannot, neither may people cross over from there to us." (Luke 16:26, NWT) So in Sheol existed two sections, one was in Abraham's bosom or paradise where the righteous awaited, and the other was where the wicked await their final judgment. It is important to note that neither of these places in Sheol or Hades is actually "Heaven" or the final Judgment of "Hell".

Although the realm of the dead is shrouded in much mystery in the revelation of the Old Testament, the New Testament is abundantly clear of where the dead were, where they are now, and where they are going to be in the future.

The Jehovah's Witness at this point may try and point to some other vague verses of Scripture throughout the Old Testament without giving any context. But what does Jesus have to say about this topic? Surely if anyone knew what happens upon death, it would be the final authority of our faith, the one who died and rose again. Jesus said that God is "not the God of the dead, but of the living", thus confirming the continual existence of Abraham, Isaac, and Jacob even after their deaths. (Matthew 22:31-32) In the Transfiguration, Jesus revealed his glory to his disciples while Moses and Elijah stood among their midst. Jesus had conversation with Moses and Elijah on the mountain of Transfiguration, thus debunking the Watchtowers claim that Moses and Elijah ceased to exist and were unconscious in the grave. (Matthew 17:1-7) However, the Watchtower contends that this was a mere "vision" and that somehow that it really wasn't Moses and Elijah there. This argument is not even serious enough to merit a response, since that would in turn make Jesus a lawbreaker for using necromancy a form of demonism to conjure up deceased spirits in apparition form. (Deuteronomy 18:11) So where are the Old Testament saints? Jesus directly said that these saints would be in Heaven, "many from eastern parts and western parts will come and recline at the table with **Abraham and Isaac and Jacob in the kingdom of the heavens**". (Matthew 8:11, NWT) Hebrews 11 refers to all the Old Testament saints as a cloud of witnesses, and verse 16 says of these saints "But now they are reaching out for a better [place], that is, **one belonging to heaven**. Hence God is not ashamed of them, to be called upon as their God, **for he has made a city ready for them**." Clearly the hope that the Old Testament saints have is to rule in God's heavenly Kingdom, the city of Zion; New Jerusalem. (Hebrews 12:22)

According to the Scriptures "it is appointed for man to die once, and after that comes judgment". (Hebrews 9:27) Unlike in Watchtower theology, the Bible states that there is some form of consciousness after death, for our Lord Jesus said "do not fear those who kill the body but cannot kill the soul. Rather fear him who can **destroy both soul and body in Gehenna**." (Matthew 10:28) When Jesus' friend Lazarus died, Jesus declared the condition of those who died believing in Him, and it is of utmost importance that we share this truth with Jehovah's Witnesses; Jesus said, "I am the resurrection and the life. He that exercises faith in me, even though he dies, will come to life; and **everyone that is living** and exercises faith in me **will never die at all**. Do you believe this?" (John 11:25-26, NWT) Jesus taught that his followers would never die, but that they would continue living. Death for the believer is not complete ruin; it is merely the separation of the body and soul. Jesus not only promises us eternal life, but that he would raise our physical bodies also.

Jesus explicitly taught that life does not end at the grave, that there was a real judgment that awaited us and not only that but he offered a way out of judgment and into life! While the Watchtower contends that eternal life with Christ is reserved for only a few, 144,000 to be exact, the New Testament is abundantly clear that there is only one hope for the Christian, and that's to be with Christ.

THE HEAVENLY CALLING

Jehovah's Witnesses have been taught that only a "little flock" of Christians will be spirit-anointed or "born again" to receive heavenly life in Christ Kingdom. In fact they believe that it is a fixed, predetermined number: 144,000. They come to this conclusion for their reading of Revelation 14:1-3 which reads as follows in the NWT: "And I saw, and, look! the Lamb standing upon the Mount Zion, and with him a **hundred and forty-four thousand** having his name and the name of his Father written on their foreheads… and no one was able to master that song **but the hundred and forty-four thousand, who have been bought from the earth.**"

Does this mean that only 144,000 will go to Heaven? Not so fast! The JW is actually reading something into this that really isn't even there. Nowhere in this verse or elsewhere in the Bible does it state that *only* 144,000 will go to Heaven. Something to bring to the attention of the JW is to point them to Revelation 7:4-8 where it states that the 144,000 are comprised of 12,000 Jews from each of the 12 tribes of Israel. The Witness will quickly try and say that it is symbolic and does not actually represent a sealing of natural Israel, but a spiritual Israel. But that's sort of the point isn't it? If we can't take the numbers of 12,000 from 12 tribes literal, why should we take the complete number of 144,000 literal? Are not most if not all the numbers in the book of Revelation symbolic in some way? There is no reason to believe that only a 144,000 Christians will rule with Christ, in fact the Bible teaches something quite the opposite.

If you want to get anywhere with the Witness in demonstrating that all believing Christians will be in God's Kingdom you will need to show them that the very group they believe will only inherit the earth, are actually going to inherit a lot more. The JW's believe that the "great crowd" in Revelation 7:9 are members of a class of Christians who will not reign with Christ, but live forever on the earth in a paradise conditions. But is there any indication that the great crowd John saw in his vision was in Heaven or on the Earth?

Notice the description the Bible gives us of the great crowd: "After these things I saw, and, look! a great crowd, which no man was able to number, out of all nations and tribes and peoples and tongues, **standing before the throne and before the Lamb,** dressed in white robes; and there were palm branches in their hands. And they keep on crying with a loud voice, saying: "Salvation [we owe] to our God, who is seated on the throne, and to the Lamb." (Revelation 7:9-10, NWT) In this passage the great crowd is said to be standing "before the throne and before the Lamb", and where exactly is the throne of God? Clearly it is in Heaven. The description of this great crowd does not end there however, John is told the identity of this massive assembly. "These are the ones that come out of the great tribulation, and they have washed their robes and made them white in the blood of the Lamb. That is why they are **before the throne of God; and they are rendering him sacred service day and night in his temple**; and the One seated on the throne will spread his tent over them." (Revelation 7:14-15, NWT)

Notice the key phrases, "before the throne" and "in his temple". At this moment you need to establish these things to the JW, that the members of the great crowd are definitely Christians who have been purchased and washed with the blood of Jesus, and thus born again. They are from every tribe, nation and language, and they render sacred worship unto God in the temple of God. Ask the JW, Where is God's temple located? You can then take them to Revelation 11:19 in their own Bible and show them that the temple in which the great crowd render worship unto Jehovah is in Heaven.

If you ever get this far with a Jehovah's Witness, it is important that you establish that there is "**one hope** to which YOU (The Christian)were called", (Ephesians 4:4, NWT) and that the Scripture warns us to not keep our "minds upon things on the earth" for "As for us, **our citizenship exists in the heavens,** from which place also we are eagerly waiting for a savior, the Lord Jesus Christ". (Philippians 3:19-20, NWT) Nowhere does the New Testament offer two distinct "hopes" for believing Christians; the only hope is that of "being with Christ, for this, to be sure, is far better", for in our case "to live is Christ, and to die, gain." (Philippians 1:21-23, NWT) Why would death be gain if we are merely unconscious in the grave, awaiting an earthly resurrection? The truth of the matter is that believers have one hope, and that's to be with Christ whether in Heaven or the Earth. The Bible teaches that the believer who dies and loses his earthly tent, we have "a building from God, a house not made with hands, everlasting in the heavens", for when "while we have our home in the body, we are absent from the Lord", but we be rather be "absent from the body and to make our home with the Lord". (2 Corinthians 5:1-8, NWT) The clear Bible teaching is that all believers go to be home with the Lord immediately upon death, where we await the resurrection of our bodies when Christ "will refashion our humiliated body to be conformed to his glorious body". (Philippians 3:21, NWT)

The Jehovah's Witnesses put themselves in incredible danger by following the men in charge of the Watchtower Society, for the leadership of Jehovah's Witnesses shuts the doors of Heaven for the majority of Witnesses. In Jesus' time there were religious elites called the Pharisees who felt that their religious righteousness opened the door to Heaven, yet excluded those beneath them. Of them Jesus said, "Woe to YOU, scribes and Pharisees, hypocrites! because YOU shut up the kingdom of the heavens before men; for YOU yourselves do not go in, neither do YOU permit those on their way in to go in." (Matthew 23:13, NWT) This is exactly what the leadership and Governing Body of Jehovah's Witnesses have done to their followers, they have taught error and lies and shut Heavens hope to millions.

PARADISE EARTH?

Jehovah's Witnesses will object to the notion that all Christians will be and actually see God and Christ. They will show you all the verses about living forever on a restored paradise earth, and ask you to explain verses like Psalm 37:4 and Matthew 5:5 which they say clearly teaches the righteous will live on the earth. Sadly, JW's don't really believe in a paradise earth. What do I mean? The Watchtower teaches that those who will inherit the earth are not actually apart of God's Kingdom, that the Kingdom is just ruling over them, thus they will never actually see or have intimate fellowship with Jehovah God and the Lord Jesus Christ. God and Jesus will always remain in the Heavens ruling over the earth, the average Jehovah's Witness has no hope or even the desire to see the God they claim to love. Growing up in the movement it never really daunted on me that I would never see God, I was taught that God can never be seen and that only the "anointed" would see God and Christ in Heaven. I can recall a time the first time I really thought about it, I was sitting in the Kingdom Hall while this very discussion was being discussed from the platform. As the brothers and sisters in the Hall were commenting on the study as they passed the microphone around, I heard how "wonderful" paradise was going to be and how Jehovah will always reign invisibly from the Heavens. Then it hit me, a sense of sadness came over me; I would forever be separated from the God I loved with all my heart. Being separated from Jehovah, this is paradise? You see when you ask the average Jehovah's Witness what they look forward to the must about the "new system of things" (aka Paradise), they will say things like "Living forever and never getting old!" or "Being able to have pet lions", and "getting to build a perfect home in the new world" or seeing dead loved ones resurrected. But I have never heard a JW or even thought to myself when I was a JW that I should be looking forward to Paradise because of God, his glory and being in perfect fellowship with our Creator. If squeezed long enough you may hear something around those lines but when it comes down to it, it really comes down to selfish motives that motivate one to live forever in the paradise. Never dying or getting old, no more sicknesses, perfect health, Paradise as taught in the Watchtower is all about man, and not about God's glory and the fellowship between God and his people.

It is interesting to note that the phrase "Paradise Earth" is nowhere to be found in Scripture. In fact most all references to "Paradise" actually refer to the Heavens in which God resides. (2 Corinthians 13:1-4; Revelation 2:7) Now I do not deny that notion of a Paradise on the Earth, I do however see a very different Paradise talked about in the Scriptures than the one presented by Jehovah's Witnesses. The truth is, the Bible does in fact talk about a restored earth and it also talks about a paradise of God. But the difference between the Watchtowers paradise and the Bibles paradise is that the Watchtower has a paradise without God, which in reality is no paradise at all.

When I began to read the Bible for myself, I was astounded at what was before me all along! Bible verses that I and countless other Witnesses have quoted at the door to door ministry actually became alive and I could finally see that the Paradise God will bring about is a Paradise where God is dwelling with his people. When the JW knocks on your door, they will likely use

Revelation 21:1-4 to highlight life in the "new system of things". The verse reads, "And I saw **a new heaven and a new earth**; for the former heaven and the former earth had passed away...I saw also the holy city, **New Jerusalem, coming down out of heaven from God** and prepared as a bride adorned for her husband. With that I heard a loud voice from the throne say: "Look! **The tent of God is with mankind, and he will reside with them**, and they will be his peoples. And **God himself will be with them**. And he will wipe out every tear from their eyes, and death will be no more, neither will mourning nor outcry nor pain be anymore. The former things have passed away." (NWT)

As the JW highlights this verse, make sure that you highlight that God's purpose for the Earth is not to merely restore it to its former state before the fall, but is to transform it or recreate the entire cosmos, where Heaven and Earth become one, and Jehovah God will dwell physically and spiritually with his people forever. The JW will be taken back by your reading of the text, because they have never been allowed to let the verse speak for its own. When I heard this explanation and I read it for myself without Watchtower lens I saw the beauty and majesty of God's ultimate purpose for the end of the age. I knew that God's true intent wasn't to be separated from his people forever, in fact that sounds a lot like the Biblical description of eternal separation in Hell, but the intent is to bring full harmony between God and man, the Heavens and the Earth. Jesus referred to it as the "re-creation, when the Son of man sits down upon his glorious throne", when Jesus as King makes all things new and brings complete harmony to the Creation realm. (Matthew 19:28; Isaiah 11:1-11)

When I was adamant defender of JW doctrines the teaching of Paradise Earth was close to my heart, it is a teaching where millions of people around the world find hope and comfort in. As you endeavor to share these precious truths with Jehovah's Witnesses, pray that God would reveal to them the true beauty of God's purpose for them, find common ground such as the Paradise, but slowly show them that the Paradise the Bible speaks of is quite literally, Heaven on Earth.

CHAPTER 13

IS HELL NOT SO HOT?

"THOSE who teach that hell is a place of torment promote a gross misrepresentation of Jehovah God and his qualities. Granted, the Bible does say that God will destroy the wicked. (2 Thessalonians 1:6-9) But righteous anger is not God's dominant quality."- *The Watchtower*, November 1st, 2008

If the doctrine of the Trinity is Jehovah's Witnesses most hatred doctrine of Christianity, than the doctrine of Hell comes in at a close second. The root of this hatred was planted in the very beginning of the Bible Students movement. Charles T. Russell, the founder of the Watchtower organization was well known for his abhorrence of the notion of Hell. Death and tragedy was a theme in young Russell's life, his mother and his 3 siblings died when he was a young boy, and he had lived to see the horrors of the American civil war. He often wondered what would be the eternal destinies of people who died and did not know God. Growing up in a Presbyterian Church, he was taught that the wicked were predestined for eternal damnation, a view that Russell just could not accept. Charles T. Russell would famously go around the Country and debate clergymen and theologians on the topic of Hell, and it was even said of Russell that he "put out the flames of Hell" with his debate performances. As we know, Russell would go on to do a Bible Study group which rejected many mainstream Christian doctrines, including Hell, and well... the rest is history.

The Jehovah's Witnesses view of Hell has always been a distinctive for them, the whole selling point of their message to Christians is that they have been lied to regarding Hell and other topics, and only they can show you the truth. The Witnesses however are not the only sect or movement who reject the traditional view of Hell, the Seventh Day Adventist, Mormons, Cristadelphians, and others maintain that Hell is merely a reference to eternal destruction. The view that the soul is not immortal and that the soul is eternally destroyed without conscious existence is a view known as Annihilationism.

In the previous chapter we learned how the Jehovah's Witnesses view death, the soul, afterlife and Heaven. We know that the Watchtower teaches that death is the end of conscious existence for human beings, and the only hope is a resurrection to a Paradise Earth. We also saw why that is not a view consistent with the Bible. Why do Jehovah's Witnesses feel so strongly against the teaching of Hell? Could the Watchtower be wrong about Hell? Did Russell really put out the flames of Hell, or do they actually still burn strong today?

GOD IS LOVE

"He that does not love has not come to know God, because **God is love**."- 1 John 4:8 NWT

One of the arguments I constantly heard against the doctrine of eternal punishment in the Kingdom Hall was that "God is love", and therefore God is incapable of administering his justice in Hellfire. My mother once told me, (I'm sure many JW's use this line) that if I ever did something really horrible, the last thing she would want to do to me is put my hand over a hot stove as punishment, so how much more would Jehovah the God of love no do that to his children. It made sense to me; I enjoyed serving a God who I knew would not send me into eternal punishment. I never gave Hell much thought as a Witness, in my worldview it didn't exist so why worry? I knew two things about Hell as a JW, 1- It wasn't real, 2- I knew I could debunk it. When the children at school or people I encountered in the ministry asked me about Hell, it was such an awesome experience to liberate people from the fear of hell, that God was love and would never create such a place of misery. People responded to that message favorably, I mean after being told your whole life you might go to hell, who wouldn't?

Many of the JW arguments against Hell stems from their view of afterlife in general, or better lack thereof. Since the Witnesses do not believe that the soul or spirit of a man continues existence after death, then obviously there is no room for an idea such as hell. If you even try to assert that the Bible may teach hell, the Jehovah Witness immediately goes into offense mode. I knew of Witnesses who would be personally offended if someone tried making an argument for hell, which is how seriously they had been trained to be opposed to it. Many Jehovah's Witnesses have inherited Charles Taze Russell's abhorrence to Hell, so much so that the very thought is offensive and ridiculous. As a JW apologist I would commonly argue from the Scriptures that hell is in violation of the nature of God, for as the verse quoted above states, "God is love", inseparable from his essence and nature. I would also point to verses that referred to death as being "sleep" (John 11:11) and verses like Ezekiel 18:4 which states that the "soul that sins, itself shall die". I also took many people to Psalm 37:9 which says that "evildoers themselves will be cut off" or "destroyed", and make the argument that God will merely "cut off" wicked people, destroy them forever, not torture them for all eternity. I often bombarded believers in hell with so many Bible verses without proper context and so rapidly that they would not have enough time to recover or answer all of my objections. And I did not intentionally give Bible verses out of context that was just how I was taught to handle the manner, although I would make the appeal that my interpretation, rather the Watchtower's interpretation was the correct context behind the verse.

But are there any legitimate reasons that a Jehovah's Witness defender, someone brought up to believe Hell was a lie from the Devil, would turn to believing in the existence of Hell? Can God be love and yet be Just? What did Jesus say about Hell? And how can you demonstrate to a Jehovah's Witness that Hell is real, and it's hot.

JESUS, HELL & GEHENNA

The average person, both Christian and Jehovah's Witness would probably be surprised to learn that Jesus spoke a lot about Hell, and I mean A LOT!

In fact, Jesus spoke more about the existence of Hell then he did Heaven. During Jesus earthly ministry the 3 big topics of his teachings revolved around first the Kingdom, secondly Hell, and thirdly money. To Jesus Hell was most certainly a real place, and I think where a lot of the confusion both for Christians and Jehovah's Witnesses stem from the distinction between Hades (Sheol) and the Greek word Jesus used in reference to Hell, Gehenna.

In JW theology Hades is the common grave, everyone who dies goes there, but Gehenna represents "eternal destruction" where there is no hope of a resurrection. The Bible however paints these places a little differently, for instance it is true that before Christ all deceased souls went into Hades with their being two distinct sections dividing the Just and unjust. (Luke 16:26) Jesus before his ascension went into Hades and when he "ascended on high he carried away captives", meaning that Christ delivered all the Old Testament saints and believers from Hades and brought them into the presence of God and opened the way for Christians to be with the Lord immediately upon death. (Ephesians 4:8-10; 1 Peter 3:19-20; Hebrews 11:13-16, 12:22-24; 2 Corinthians 5:7) Hades is now a waiting place of Judgment, and those in Hades will rise on the last day to give an account to God and all those who are not found in the Lambs book of life will indeed face Hell, the lake of fire. (Revelation 20:12-15) Gehenna is a word used by Jesus in the New Testament Gospels to describe what the Book of Revelation calls the "lake of fire" or the "second death". In fact, almost every modern translation of the Bible with the exception of the King James Version, translates only 'Gehenna' as 'Hell' and they do not translate 'Hades' as Hell. Jehovah's Witnesses rightly bring up that the word 'Gehenna' means "Valley of Hinnom", a literal place in ancient times that was used as a garbage field in which it was customary to dispose of the bodies of the poor and criminals, and because it was a place of waste there was always a fire burning, and it was notoriously filled with worms and creatures feasting on the decaying filth. Jehovah's Witnesses believe that Jesus used Gehenna as a metaphor of eternal destruction instead of eternal damnation. But what did Jesus actually say about hell?

Jesus said "it is finer for you to enter into life maimed than with two hands to go off into **Gehenna, into the fire that cannot be put out**...it is finer for you to enter into life lame than with two feet to be **pitched into Gehenna**. And if your eye makes you stumble, throw it away; it is finer for you to enter one-eyed into the kingdom of God than with two eyes to be pitched into Gehenna, **where their maggot does not die and the fire is not put out**." (Mark 9:43-48, NWT) Jesus could not make the reality of

Hell more clearly, he directly points to Gehenna as a place of judgment for sin, it is the opposite of the kingdom of God, and it is very real in the eyes of Jesus. Christ constantly taught that Gehenna or Hell was directly linked to judgment, for instance, "However, I say to YOU that everyone who continues wrathful with his brother **will be accountable to the court of justice**; but whoever addresses his brother with an unspeakable word of contempt **will be accountable to the Supreme Court**; whereas whoever says, 'You despicable fool!' will be **liable to the fiery Gehenna**." (Matthew 5:22, NWT) Jesus equates Gehenna with judgment, which just does not make any sense if those who go into Gehenna are unconscious eternally, for there has been no accountability for their actions, and ultimately no judgment or justice. We find various visions of Hell through the teachings and parables of Jesus, such as we find in Matthew chapter 13. Jesus in his interpretation of his parable of the wheat and the weeds explained the condition of the wicked after his judgment; "just as the weeds are collected and burned with fire, **so it will be** in the conclusion of the system of things. The Son of man will send forth his angels, and they will collect out from his kingdom all things that cause stumbling and persons who are doing lawlessness, and they will **pitch them into the fiery furnace**. There is where [their] weeping and the gnashing of [their] teeth will be." (Matthew 13:40-42, NWT)

Our Lord also taught that Death is not the worst punishment for sins, rather he said, "Do not fear those who **kill the body** and **after this are not able to do anything more**. But I will indicate to YOU whom to fear: Fear him who after killing **has authority to throw into Gehenna**. Yes, I tell YOU, fear this One." (Luke 12:4-5, NWT)

The only argument the Witnesses have regarding the dozens of texts like this one is that they are all "symbolic" of eternal destruction, without giving any exegesis of the text. Notice however that this passage is an explanation of a parable; he is explaining the meaning and identity of the sower, the enemy and the seeds and also the destinies of the 'weeds' and the 'wheat'. Jesus clearly said those who practice lawlessness will be pitched into the fiery furnace will they will experience "weeping and gnashing of teeth", which is inconsistent with the view of Annihilationism. We see the contrast in verse 43 of Matthew 13 for those who believe, "the righteous ones will shine as brightly as the sun in the kingdom of their Father. Let him that has ears listen." We need to urge Jehovah's Witnesses with all truth and sincerity to heed Jesus' words, and pray that they would ears to listen. In fact, in case Jesus wasn't making himself perfectly clear in his explanation of the parable, he continues, "That is how it will be in the conclusion of the system of things: the angels will go out and **separate the wicked** from among the righteous and will **cast them into the fiery furnace**. There is where [their] weeping and the gnashing of [their] teeth will be." (Matthew 13:49-50, NWT)

It is clear that Jesus believed and taught about Hell, he said that it is a real place of torment likened to fire, darkness and gnashing of teeth. There are so many instances and verses where Jesus is teaching on this topic, but I want to look at one more instance where Jesus talks about the place we call Hell. In Matthew 25 Jesus is teaching his disciples about the Great Judgment that will come at the end of the age, the Judgment in which He himself is the Judge over. Jesus refers to throwing the "good-for-nothing slave out into the darkness outside" and that when he arrives in glory and sits on his judgment throne "all the nations will be gathered before him, and he will separate people one from another, just as a shepherd separates the sheep from the goats. And he will put the sheep on his right hand, but the goats on his left." (Matthew 25:30-33, NWT) To the sheep in his right hand he gives the inheritance of the Father's kingdom, and to those on his left he departs and says "YOU who have been cursed, into the **everlasting fire prepared for the Devil and his angels**...And these will depart into **everlasting cutting-off**, but the righteous ones into **everlasting life**." (Matthew 25:41-46, NWT)

Notice that these verses are clearly talking about punishment and reward, yet in the New World Translation from which I quoted from, the translators used the phrase "everlasting cutting-off" instead the "eternal punishment" as seen in most Bible translations. The JW will point to that and say that his translation says cutting-off and not punishment, and that our Bibles were translated by bias scholars who are trying to promote the idea of Hell to keep their Church members scared straight! The Witness has been conditioned to exalt their NWT Bible as superior anytime there is a major doctrinally significant reading of certain verses. This is one of those instances, where the Watchtower has taken the Greek word "kólasis" and has changed its 1st century meaning. Is the NWT just a superior translation, or is the Watchtower actually the bias translator? When the NWT was originally translated, the Watchtower Society had already been teaching that Hell was nonexistence for nearly 70 years. So no doubt they fashioned a "Bible translation" that fit their theology not just on this topic but many others including the deity of Christ. For instance the Greek word they translated as "cutting-off" (kólasis) literally means according to the widely accepted Strong's Exhaustive Concordance, "**correction, punishment, penalty**...brings with it or has connected with it the thought of punishment." Nearly every New Testament Greek Lexicon and Concordance agrees that "kólasis" rightly means "punishment" and not simply "cutting-off".

They mistranslate the word to try and detract from what our Lord Jesus was saying, the reality that he was stating, that there is a Judgment and penalty for sin. This has been a surreal and sobering chapter to write as an ex-Jehovah's Witness. There are so many implications to Hell being a clear and defined Bible teaching, but I guess the next question the Witness would ask is why? Why would God create and send human beings created in his image to a place or torment and separation?

GOD IS JUST

God is love, therefore he is just. Our Creator has a greater sense of justice than any human being can ever have. Hell exists because God will not force anyone into his Kingdom, but he still demands a payment for sins. Just as if we were to break the laws of the land in which we lived and stood before the judge and human court, the judge would hold us accountable whether or not you want to be held accountable. Why is that? Because that is just and morally right. Imagine what kind of a God would tolerate murder, genocide, rape, racism, injustice and corruption by allowing the wicked men who do it to escape judgment by enjoying sleep for all eternity? The Bible says "The Rock, his work is perfect; For all his ways are justice: A God of faithfulness and without iniquity, Just and right is he." (Deuteronomy 32:4, ASV) Because God is love, God must also be perfectly just, and there is a penalty and ultimate judgment for sins. Romans 6:23 says that the penalty of "sin is death", which is eternal separation from God in Gehenna, the place which Jesus taught us to fear. (Luke 12:4-5) The Jehovah's Witness needs to understand the gravity and seriousness of our transgression and condition before God. The Witness acknowledges we are all sinful, but they believe we are also good and can choose to follow Jehovah. The Bible however states "There is **not a righteous** **[man], not even one**; there is no one that has any insight, there is **no one** **that seeks for God**." (Romans 3:10-11, NWT) Man in his fallen condition is so depraved that in our fallen nature, no man seeks after God. Because of this, God's wrath abides on mankind, for as it is written "Whoever believes in the Son has eternal life; whoever does not obey the Son shall not see life, but the **wrath of God remains on him.**" (John 3:36, ESV) The Jehovah's Witness needs to come to grips that their sinful condition is a lot worse than they have been taught. They also need to see the seriousness of sin in the eyes of God and that their denial of God's judgment does not negate the fact that it is real. The Jehovah's Witnesses live in constant denial and are in turn storing up wrath for themselves. "But according to your **hardness** and **unrepentant heart** you are **storing up wrath** for yourself on the **day of wrath** and of the revealing of God's righteous judgment." (Romans 2:5, NWT)

While it is true that the Bible uses terms like the wicked being cut off, death being likened to sleep and Hell as eternal destruction, which leads the Witness to believe that Hell is nonexistence. But as we examined, the Scriptures clearly teach that there is existence after the grave, and that the references of death as sleep is referring to the condition of the human body which decays and asleep until the resurrection at the last day. (John 11:11-24; Acts 2:29) If you point the Jehovah's Witness to the Bible and show them that God's Word does not support the notion of a wicked person simply dying and not receiving judgment. 2 Corinthians 5:10 we are confronted with the reality that "we must **all** appear before the **judgment seat of Christ**, that each one may **receive what is due him** for the things **done while in the body,** whether good or bad." Clearly death is not an escape of God's judgment, and the Watchtower actually teaches that some that die are so wicked that they will not even be resurrected in the last day to face judgment; there punishment is never being resurrected. A question to ask the Witness at that point is, if that is so than why does the Bible say that **all** will stand before the throne of Christ? Revelation 20:12-13 says in the NWT, "And I saw the dead, **the great and the small,** standing before the throne, and scrolls were opened. But another scroll was opened; it is the scroll of life. And **the dead were judged** out of those things written in the scrolls **according to their deeds.** And the sea gave up those dead in it, and death and Hades gave up those dead in them, and they were **judged individually** according to their deeds." Each person in Hades, every single person who has ever lived, good or bad, will face God in the great white throne of judgment, including every single Jehovah's Witness who has ever lived and died. And what happens to those not found in the Lamb's book of life? "And death and Hades were hurled into the lake of fire. This means the second death, the lake of fire. Furthermore, whoever was not found written in the book of life was **hurled into the lake of fire.**" (Revelation 20:14-15, NWT)

Friends, it is of eternal importance that we believe and lovingly share with the Jehovah's Witness the reality of God's love and justice, and that they see that their eternal souls are at risk! The JW focuses on the part of that verse where it mentions that the lake of fire is the "second death", and argue that the second death is death without hope of a resurrection. But that is simply not right, for our Lord Jesus himself said that the "time is coming when **all** who are in the graves will hear His voice and come out—those who have done good things, to the **resurrection of life**, but those who have done **wicked things**, to the **resurrection of judgment**." (John 5:28-29, HCSB)

The Jehovah's Witness needs to be shown that God will not allow sin and iniquity to go unpunished, and that the good news of Jesus Christ is that through his death, burial and resurrection our fine has been paid, our debt has been cleared if we repent and turn to Jesus for the forgiveness of sins. (Acts 10:36-43) Jesus said he came down to give his life as a ransom in exchange for many. God can legally dismiss our case by Jesus Christ being our mediator and advocate. (1 Timothy 2:5-6) The Jehovah's Witness is in desperate need of Jesus Christ as their Savior and mediator, if they continue to believe the lies the Watchtower Society teaches, they will undoubtedly receive the mark of the beast and will "drink of the wine of the **anger of God** that is poured out undiluted into the **cup of his wrath**, and he **shall be tormented with fire and sulphur** in the sight of the holy angels and in the sight of the Lamb. And the smoke of their **torment ascends forever and ever**, and **day and night they have no rest**". (Revelation 14:10-11, NWT) This does not sound like the condition of unconscious human beings; this is a real judgment and a just judgment.

Hell is not a place where Satan is ruling over and is torturing people, God created Hell as a place for Satan and his disobedient Angels to be subjected to eternal destruction and punishment. (2 Peter 2:4; Jude 6) The Scripture says that Satan will be hurled into the lake of fire and "will be tormented day and night forever and ever." (Revelation 20:10) Remember Jesus said that God prepared Hell for the Devil and his angels, yet because mankind has followed after Satan their destiny will be the same. (Matthew 25:41, 46) In Hell the judgment is eternal, the death is eternal, and the punishment is eternal. The Scriptures warn us of following after twisted men who twist the Scriptures for their own purposes, and the Governing Body of Jehovah's Witnesses fit this description perfectly. Charles T Russell was wrong, and the men who have taken the lead in the organization he founded have continued in his error. Of them it is written that they are like "rocks hidden below water in YOUR love feasts while they feast with YOU, **shepherds that feed themselves without fear; waterless clouds** carried this way and that by winds; trees in late autumn, but fruitless, having died twice, having been uprooted; wild waves of the sea that foam up their own causes for shame; stars with no set course, for which **the blackness of darkness stands reserved forever.**" (Jude 12-13, NWT)

Please pray for the Jehovah's Witnesses in your life, for they are unaware of the real danger of their sins and rebellion against Jehovah God. This has not been an easy subject for me, as I researched the material for this chapter, the heavier my heart felt for my loved ones and family members who are in the Watchtower Society. I often time feel the frustration and the urgency in the rich man who died and woke up in Hades being in torment, begging that someone would send a messenger to his father's house to warn them the reality of God's judgment and that they would they would receive a "thorough witness, that they also should not get into this place of torment." (Luke 16:22-28, NWT)

It is my prayer that God would in this case be merciful and sends my beloved Jehovah's Witness family members a witness, whether through me or any other Christian they may encounter. I pray that when my father, mother, brother and sister knock on the door of a Christian, the Christian will be ready to share, love and proclaim. Can I *please* get a witness?

"He that hears my word and believes him that sent me has everlasting life, and he does not come into **judgment** but has passed over from **death to life**."- Jesus, John 5:24 NWT

Chapter 14

The Physical Resurrection & Return of Christ

The bodily resurrection of Christ is the core of the Gospel of Jesus. Christianity makes or breaks on the validity of Christ bodily resurrection and his claim that he will come again. So important is the resurrection of Jesus Christ that the apostle Paul wrote, "if Christ has not been raised, your faith is futile; you are still in your sins. Then those also who have fallen asleep in Christ are lost. If only for this life we have hope in Christ, we are of all people most to be pitied." (1 Corinthians 15:17-19, NIV) The word "resurrection" literally means a "standing up again", or a "rising again". The Christian faith rests on the assurance that Jesus Christ stood up and rose over death and the grave.

The Jehovah's Witnesses believe that Jesus Christ died on a torture stake and was recreated or resurrected as a spirit creature 3 days later, the body that Jesus died in was forever lost. Charles T Russell wrote concerning the body of our Lord, "...the man **Jesus is dead, forever dead**..." (*The Atonement Between God and Man, Studies in the Scriptures*, 1899). I use the word "recreated" in connection to the Watchtower's teaching on Christ resurrection because in WT theology Jesus ceased to exist when he died on the torture stake. Jesus, even as Russell wrote, was "forever dead", for the soul and spirit of Jesus ceased to exist upon death. Thus, Jehovah God had to "recreate" Jesus from his perfect memory, and bring him back as a spirit creature. The Witnesses believe that Jesus "was the first ever to be resurrected to everlasting life. And his resurrection was "in the spirit," to life in heaven. (1Pe 3:18)... He was granted immortality and incorruption, which no creature in the flesh can have". (*Insight*, Volume 2) What evidence do they have to claim that Jesus was resurrected as a spirit without his physical body?

The Witnesses point to Bible verses such as 1 Peter 3:18, which reads in the NWT: "Christ died once for all time concerning sins, a righteous [person] for unrighteous ones, that he might lead YOU to God, he being put to **death in the flesh**, but being made **alive in the spirit**." And 1 Corinthians 15:45 in the NWT: "The first man Adam became a living soul." The last Adam became a **life-giving spirit**." On the basis of these two Scriptures, the JW's that the resurrection of Jesus was not bodily or physical, but spiritual. What about the post-resurrection appearances where Jesus physically appeared to his disciples and even to a crowd of 500? The Watchtower Society responds as follows: "However, for 40 days after his resurrection Jesus appeared to his disciples on different occasions in various fleshly bodies, just as angels had appeared to men of ancient times. Like those angels, he had the power to construct and to disintegrate those fleshly bodies at will, for the purpose of proving visibly that he had been resurrected. (Mt 28:8-10, 16-20; Lu 24:13-32, 36-43; Joh 20:14-29; Ge 18:1, 2; 19:1; Jos 5:13-15; Jg 6:11, 12; 13:3, 13) His many appearances, and particularly his manifesting himself to more than 500 persons at one time, provide strong testimony to the truth of his resurrection. (1Co 15:3-8)" (*Insight*, Volume 2)

So in a nutshell, JW's believe that Jesus materialized different bodies to convince his disciples that he had truly resurrected. So in effect, Jesus had to mislead his followers into believing that he was raised from the dead. Nonetheless, when I was a Witness this was yet another doctrine I accepted only because it was what I was taught, and there were two Bible verses to back it up. Good enough for the average Witness, it was good enough for me at the time as well. Remember, JW's are very doctrinally isolated from the rest of the World, I didn't even know that this was a big deal or that or Christian faiths believed otherwise. The only time I knew about other religions beliefs were when we met people of various religions in the ministry, and when the

Watchtower printed material trying to refute the viewpoints of other faiths. But as I began to become more active in defending my JW faith online, the topic of the resurrection of Christ was no longer a topic that I could merely ignore. I began researching exactly why I believed that Jesus was raised a spirit creature in order to defend my faith, even making a video on YouTube defending the Watchtowers position on the matter. Not only did I appeal to 1 Peter 3:18 and 1 Corinthians 15:45, but I also would point out that during the resurrection appearances, many mistook or did not fully recognize Jesus, evidence that Jesus was materializing bodies. (John 20:14-20) The Witnesses also reason that since Jesus offered up his body in the ransom sacrifice, that it would be counterintuitive for God to give Jesus back the same body that Jesus had just offered. So what does the Bible really teach about the nature of the resurrection of Jesus Christ?

A GLORIOUS RESURRECTION

So what convinced this devout Jehovah's Witness that Jesus had been raised in a glorious physical body? What about those two proof texts that say Jesus was raised "in the spirit"? The Bible is actually abundantly clear as to the nature of Christ resurrection, and it's a glorious one. First, there is no verse in all of Scripture that says Christ was "resurrected as a spirit"; second, there is no verse that ever says that Jesus "materialized" bodies at his post-resurrection appearances. 1 Peter 3:18 for instance very easily seems to be a reference to the Holy Spirit's role in the resurrection of Christ, for the New International Version translates that verse as, "He was put to death in the body but made **alive in the Spirit**", with "the Spirit" being the Holy Spirit. This would be in harmony with Romans 1:4 which states that "through the **Spirit of holiness** (Jesus) was appointed the Son of God in power by **his resurrection from the dead**: Jesus Christ our Lord." (NIV) And Romans 8:11 which says "If **the Spirit of him who raised Jesus from the dead** dwells in you, he who raised Christ Jesus from the dead will also give life to your **mortal bodies** through his Spirit who dwells in you." (ESV) 1 Peter 3:18 is actually pointing, not to the nature or essence of the resurrection of Jesus, but to the transforming power behind it. In this context, 1 Corinthians 15:45 is not a problem either, for Adam in this verses is said to be a "living soul" yet it would be silly to deny that Adam had a fleshly body, so too it would be wrong to assume that Jesus does not possess a glorified physical body just because he is a "life-giving spirit". Does the Bible actually say that Jesus was raised with a glorified physical body? Yes. First let's examine the Gospel accounts of Jesus' resurrection. After Christ appeared to a few of the disciples after his resurrection, the disciples went on to tell the other believers and to Thomas, but Thomas was not convinced. "So the other disciples were saying to him, "We have seen the Lord!" But he said to them, "Unless I see in His hands the imprint of the nails, and put my finger into the place of the nails, and put my hand into His side, I will not believe." (John 20:25, NASB) Thomas is looking for physical evidence, he wants to touch and see the crucified body of Christ. Jesus appears to Thomas and says, "Reach here with your finger, and see My hands; and reach here your hand and put it into My side; and do not be unbelieving, but believing." (John 20:27, NASB) Jesus was in the same body that was hanged upon the Cross, it does not say that He materialized a body that was similar to the one on the Cross.

Even more devastating to the JW view that Jesus was resurrected as a spirit, is in the resurrection appearance account found in Luke 24:37-40: "But they were startled and frightened and thought that they were seeing a **spirit**. And He said to them, "Why are you troubled, and why do doubts arise in your hearts? See **My hands** and **My feet**, that it is **I Myself**; touch Me and see, for **a spirit does not have flesh and bones as you see that I have.**" And when He had said this, He showed them His hands and His feet." (NASB) Unless Jesus was purposely misleading his disciples, it is clear that Christ himself was demonstrating that his resurrection was a literal "standing up again" of the flesh that was nailed to the Cross.

Acts 13:34-37 is fascinating when speaking to the Witnesses about Christ resurrection. The verse reads in the HCSB version of the Bible: "Since He (God) raised Him (Jesus) from the dead, never to return to **decay**, He has spoken in this way, 'I will grant you the faithful covenant blessings made to David'. Therefore He also says in another passage, 'You will not allow Your Holy One to see decay'. For David, after serving his own generation in God's plan, fell asleep, was buried with his fathers, and **decayed**. But the **One God raised up did not decay.**" In this passage we see the promise God had made regarding the Messiah who came from the line of David regarding the resurrection. The promise was that Messiahs body would not see corruption or decay in Death, King David's body is buried and has decayed, however the body of Christ did not decay or see corruption for it was raised up. The Jehovah's Witnesses believe that the body of Jesus was destroyed by Jehovah God, yet there is no Scripture that says that, in fact it says the opposite, that Christ body would not experience decay because of the fact that it would be raised.

When sharing these Bible verses with the Jehovah's Witnesses, they will be quick to point to the Bible verses where Mary and the disciples did not recognize Jesus, thus according to their reasoning, proving that Jesus "materialized" different bodies to convince them that he had truly risen. For instance in John 20:14-15 Mary mistakes Jesus for the Gardener, so does this prove that Jesus materialized the body of a gardener? At one time the disciples were debating and walking from a village called Emmaus, and Jesus began walking with them but the Scripture explains that "their **eyes were kept from recognizing him**". (Luke 24:16, NWT) By God's supernatural power, Christ kept their eyes from recognizing him; it was not that he was materializing different bodies. Why did Jesus keep them from recognizing him? The disciples at that time still did not understand why the Messiah had to suffer, die and be resurrected to life, even though Jesus himself had predicted and warned of these events beforehand, and they "did not understand" what he was saying. (Mark 9:31-32) If the disciples would have recognized Jesus, they would have been too excited or emotional to understand the significance of this event in the Scriptures. So "commencing at Moses and all the Prophets he interpreted to them things pertaining to himself in all the Scriptures." (Luke 24:27, NWT) Jesus taught them the Word and opened their eyes to the Scriptures, before finally sitting with them and revealing himself as "their eyes were fully opened and they recognized him". (Luke 24:31, NWT) The disciples were not allowed to see Jesus physically until they could see him or understand him spiritually. That is why the disciples responded by saying, "Were not our hearts burning as he was speaking to us on the road, as he was fully opening up the Scriptures to us?" And in that very hour they rose and returned to Jerusalem... saying: "For a fact the Lord was raised up and he appeared to Simon!" (Luke 24:32-34, NWT) Jesus did not materialize bodies to convince the disciples he had risen, for he had risen in the same body that was hung upon that tree, a glorious spiritual body. Concerning the topic of how the dead are raised, the apostle Paul wrote: "How are the dead to be raised up? Yes, with what sort of body are they coming? ... And there are **heavenly bodies**, and **earthly bodies**; but the glory of the heavenly bodies is one sort, and that of the earthly bodies is a different sort... So also is the resurrection of the dead. **It** is sown in corruption, **it is raised up in incorruption**. It is sown in dishonor, **it is raised up in glory**. It is sown in weakness, **it is raised up in power**. It is sown a physical body, it is raised up a **spiritual body**. If there is a physical body, there is also a spiritual one." (1 Corinthians 15:35-44, NWT) The JW's believe that Paul's reference to the "spiritual bodies" mean an immaterial body, the absence of the physical. However that is not what Paul is saying at all, for he referring to our lowly bodies says "it is sown in dishonor, it is raised up in glory". (1 Corinthians 15:43, NWT) The "it" is in reference to the human body which is sown in dishonor, which is the same human body which will be raised up in glory. So believers will share in the same kind of resurrection as Jesus, for Jesus himself is the "first fruits" from the dead, for "if we have been joined with Him in the likeness of His death, we will certainly also be in the likeness of His resurrection." (Romans 6:5, HCSB; 1 Corinthians 15:20) There is only one type of resurrection in Scripture, and that is a bodily one. The JW's believe that since Jesus was raised as a spirit creature, that the 144,000 "anointed" Christians will also be raised as spirit creatures, and the rest of faithful Witnesses will be resurrected bodily. However there is no verse in all of Scripture that refers to a bodily resurrection and a spirit resurrection. There is one type, and Jesus is the foreshadowing of that resurrection.

This former Jehovah's Witness was convinced by the overwhelming testimony of Jesus Christ and the rest of Scripture of the glorious and bodily resurrection of Jesus. The resurrection of Jesus is the most glorious event in all of History, and the awesome part of this resurrection is that this former Jehovah's Witness who grew up with no hope or desire to ever be with Jesus, will not only be with Jesus but will share in the resurrection of Jesus! "As for us, **our citizenship exists in the heavens**, from which place also we are eagerly waiting for a savior, the **Lord Jesus Christ**, who will **refashion** our **humiliated body** to be **conformed** to **his glorious body** according to the operation of the power that he has, even to subject all things to himself." (Philippians 3:20-21, NWT) Praise God!

WHO RESURRECTED CHRIST?

This topic on the resurrection of Jesus also raises a big question, who exactly resurrected Christ? If the Jehovah's Witnesses become frustrated they will jump unto a topic they feel they have the upper hand in, so if you demonstrated with them that Christ really rose bodily, then the next question is "Well who raised Christ?" Obviously the Witnesses believe that Jehovah God, the

Father resurrected Christ, and they would be right in that. Where they are wrong however, is that they believe that Jesus had no role whatsoever in his own resurrection. Remember, in WT theology Jesus ceased to exist upon death, the Witnesses always say "a dead man cannot raise himself". But what does the Bible really teach concerning who resurrected Christ Jesus?

It is certainly true, God the Father had a role in resurrecting Jesus Christ, for it is written that "God has resurrected this Jesus. We are all witnesses of this." (Acts 13:32, HCSB) However, Jesus said that He would be responsible and had the authority for his own resurrection from the dead. When speaking with the Jews, the Jews demanded a sign of the authenticity of Jesus' ministry. Jesus responded by saying, "Break down this temple, and in three days **I will raise it up.**" The Jews responded dumbfounded for they understood Jesus was claiming to overthrow the beloved Temple, the center of Jewish worship in Jerusalem. Yet this is not what Christ was talking about, instead "he was talking about the **temple of his body.** When, though, he **was raised up from the dead,** his disciples called to mind that he used to say this; and they believed the Scripture and the saying that Jesus said." (John 2:18-22, NWT) Jesus clearly said that He would "raise it up", the temple of His body. This demonstrates both that Christ raised himself from the dead, and that it was the temple of His **body** that He raised! As if this very explicit verse does not convince the average JW, Jesus made another compelling case for His authority to raise himself from the dead. Jesus said: ""For this reason the Father loves Me, because I lay down My life so that **I may take it again.** No one has taken it away from Me, but I lay it down on **My own initiative. I have authority** to lay it down, and **I have authority to take it up again.** This commandment I received from My Father." (John 10:17-18, NASB) Jesus claims absolute authority over the receiving up of his own resurrection, it is in fact a commandment from the Father that Christ would have dominion over His resurrection. The Jehovah's Witnesses will be quick to object and say how unreasonable it would be for Christ to resurrect himself, and will point to the Bible verses that it was God the Father that raised Jesus. Is there a contradiction? No, for the fullness of the Trinity, Father, Son and Holy Spirit were active in the resurrection of the Lord Jesus Christ. The Father raised Jesus, (Acts 5:30) Jesus raised himself, (John 2:19-22) and the Holy Spirit raised Jesus. (Romans 1:4) Concerning the Holy Spirits role in the resurrection of Jesus, Romans 8:11 proclaims that the Holy Spirit directly raised Jesus from the dead. We see each member of the Godhead active and participating in Christ glorious resurrection from the dead.

"EVERY EYE WILL SEE HIM"

40 days after Christ resurrection, Jesus had left the Apostles and disciples many proofs that He had risen from the grave, and now He was poised to return to His God and Father in the Heavenly realm. But his departure was not without a promise, He would return again. As the disciples gazed upon the resurrected Christ ascending into Heaven, two angels stood by them and said, "This Jesus who was received up from YOU into the sky will come thus in the same manner as YOU have beheld him going into the sky." (Acts 1:11, NWT) The Jehovah's Witness believe and teach that Jesus Christ has already "returned" invisibly to rule over God's kingdom. JW's refer to Christ second coming as his "parousia" which is the Greek word for "arrival or coming" and is translated as "presence" in the New World Translation. They believe that the "parousia" or coming of the Lord is not a one-time event, but a period of time. In the book *"The Truth Shall Set You Free"* published by Jehovah's Witnesses in 1943 said, "The King's presence or *parousia* began in 1914, and then his appearing or *epiphaneia* at the temple came in 1918." Before that time the Witnesses actually taught that Jesus' return or presence began in 1874, but later changed it to 1914. The Witnesses nonetheless have been consistent in their belief that Christ would be forever invisible to the human eye, and that his return would be in secret, with little fanfare or visible signs. In Watchtower theology there are 3 stages of Christ "presence", the first being Christ installment as King which they claim occurred in 1914. The second is the "arrival" or inspection where Christ appoints his "faithful slave", which until recently they believed it already happened in the year 1918, now they are saying it is a still future event. The third and final stage of Christ "presence" is when Jesus "comes back" invisibly as God's executioner at Armageddon. The Witnesses, however, feel that they have Biblical grounds to believe that Christ return would be invisible, for Jesus himself said, "A little longer and the **world will behold me no more**, but YOU will behold me, because I live and YOU will live." (John 14:19, NWT) Since the JW's believe that Jesus was resurrected as an invisible spirit creature they reason that his return would also have to be invisible. So are the JW's right and the return of Christ is actually invisible?

According to the testimony of Christ, the answer is no. Jesus was perfectly clear and left no room for doubt regarding his arrival, and even told us to reject voices which would say that only they have a special knowledge of Christ return. "Then if anyone says to YOU, 'Look! **Here is the Christ**,' or,

'There!' do not believe it. For false Christ's and **false prophets will arise** and will give great signs and wonders so as to mislead, if possible, even the chosen ones. Look! I have forewarned YOU. Therefore, if people say to YOU, 'Look! **He is in the wilderness,**' do not go out; 'Look! **He is in the inner chambers,**' **do not believe it.**" (Matthew 24:23-26, NWT) Jehovah's Witnesses claim to have special revelation that they alone know about, that Christ Jesus returned invisibly, in effect they proclaim, "Look! He is already Here!" Jesus said to not even go after such a person. Christ said that his return would be so palpable, so clear that he likened it to lightening flashing. "For just as the lightning comes out of eastern parts and shines over to western parts, so the presence (arrival, coming) of the Son of man will be." (Matthew 24:27, NWT) Jesus' Second coming isn't a quiet, secret affair, it is very public and will be very visible. Our Lord said that after the great tribulation, "the sign of the Son of man will appear in heaven, and then all the tribes of the earth will beat themselves in lamentation, and they will **see the Son of man coming** on the clouds of heaven with power and great glory." (Matthew 24:30, NWT) The Second coming is a visible, not an invisible event!

The rest of the Bible is also pretty consistent in the visible manner of Christ return. For instance the Colossians 3:4 says, "When **Christ,** who is your life, **appears,** then you also will appear with him in glory." (NIV) And Titus 2:13 says that "we wait for **the blessed hope** - the **glorious appearing** of our great God and Savior, Jesus Christ". (NIV) The visible and physical return of Christ is the blessed hope all true Christians look forward to. If 1914 was the "blessed hope", then I am sorry that all we got was a World War and a major influenza. With regard to those two verses I quoted, the New World Translation does not use the word "appear" or "appearing", rather it uses the words "manifest" and "manifestation". Even if that translation of the word, it does not derail from the fact that the appearing or manifestation is visible and noticeable to those on the Earth. Then what about the Bible verse, John 14:19 where Jesus said the World would see him no longer? In the light of the rest of Scripture, and in harmony with the immediate context, Jesus was talking about his death, resurrection and ascension, not his return. Jesus said that in a little longer the World would no longer behold him, because he was going to die, be raised and ascend to his Father, so his earthly ministry was ending. No longer would Jesus be around to preach to the masses, heal the sick and raise the dead. But he also said "You will behold me, because I live, you will live also", so Jesus was talking about those who follow Him would also live with Him. But Jesus did not mean that he would forever be invisible and return invisibly, for we know that Christ was raised with a supernatural body and will return bodily, not as an invisible spirit. Jesus on numerous occasions said that his return would be seen and visible. (Matthew 26:64; Mark 8:36-38; Luke 21:25-28) Who are we going to trust?

The testimony of Holy Scripture is sure, "Look! He is coming with the clouds, **and every eye will see him**, and those who pierced him; and all the tribes of the earth will beat themselves in grief because of him. Yes, Amen" (Revelation 1:7, NWT) The last line of defense in the apologetic of the Jehovah's Witness in regard to these verses, especially Revelation 1:7 is that it is symbolic, and that "every eye" will see Jesus with "their mind of understanding". So in other words, the Watchtower claims that by the physical events surrounding the final stage of Christ "presence" when he comes as God's executioner at Armageddon, everyone will know or understand that somehow it is an invisible Jesus behind all of those events. This argument is neither found in Scripture nor logical. Jesus went out of his way to teach that his return would be visibly seen, his return is the hope of the universe and along with the resurrection, the bedrock of our Christian message. Pray that the Jehovah's Witnesses in your life would take the words of Jesus to heart, and obey Him rather than men, that they would repent before the glorious coming of the Lord. We pray that they would like the ones who "turned to God from idols to serve **the living and true God**, and **to wait for his Son from heaven**, whom he raised from the dead - **Jesus, who rescues us from the coming wrath**." (1 Thessalonians 1:9) May we find comfort in the glorious resurrection of Jesus, and find hope in His coming again.

"Behold, **I am coming soon**! My reward is with me, and I will give to everyone according to what he has done. I am the Alpha and the Omega, the First and the Last, the Beginning and the End... He who testifies to these things says, "Yes, **I am coming soon**." Amen, **Come, Lord Jesus**. The grace of the Lord Jesus be with God's people. Amen."- Revelation 22:12-13, 20

CHAPTER 15

THE GOSPEL DIFFERENCE

"I am amazed that you are so quickly turning away from Him who called you by the grace of Christ and are turning to a different gospel- not that there is another gospel, but there are some who are troubling you and want to **change** the *good news* about the Messiah." (Galatians 1:6, HCSB) The word "Gospel" literally means a declaration of "good news" or tithing's. To Paul who penned those words to the Galatians, it was of utmost importance to have a correct understanding of the Good news of Jesus. And with those words the Apostle Paul gave a warning to the Church in Galatia that many were turning to a different gospel a gospel not based upon the calling of God through the grace of Christ. Having the correct message is of eternal significance. What are some of the major differences between the "good news" that Jehovah's Witnesses zealously bring door to door and the Good news of the Bible?

THE WATCHTOWER GOSPEL

The Watchtower Society acknowledges that the gospel preached by Christians and the one preached by their members are two very distinct messages.

The Society writes; "Let the honest-hearted person compare the kind of preaching of the gospel of the Kingdom done by the religious systems of Christendom during all the centuries with that done by Jehovah's Witnesses since the end of World War I in 1918. **They are not one and the same kind.**" How exactly does the JW gospel differ from the Christian gospel? The Watchtower explains, "That of Jehovah's Witnesses is really "gospel," or "good news," as of God's heavenly **kingdom that was established** by the enthronement of his Son Jesus Christ at the **end of the Gentile Times in** 1914." (*The Watchtower*, May 1ˢᵗ, 1981)

The Gospel according to the Watchtower is that God enthroned his Son Jesus as King of his Kingdom in the year 1914. The Witnesses give lip service by saying that the "Good news" they preach is the same Kingdom message that Jesus Christ and the disciples preached. But the gospel according to the Watchtower is not talking about the same Kingdom message as Jesus, for the Kingdom message by Jehovah's Witnesses is that God established his Kingdom in the year 1914. This is a far cry from the message preached by Jesus.

In my experience, I grew up with the impression that only we, only Jehovah's Witnesses were out there preaching the Kingdom message. I felt my religion was vindicated in that only we went door to door, to market places, street corners, preaching "the Good news of the Kingdom". I rarely saw other religious groups making the sacrifice to publish and proclaim their religions message as vigorous as we did. The Mormon Church sends out young missionaries, about 51,000 worldwide, but that pales in comparison to an army of 7 million "Kingdom publishers". I was taught that our Kingdom proclamation was a mark of us being the true religion, that we alone were True Christians.

But in reality, Jehovah's Witnesses do not even preach their version of the "Good news of the Kingdom". What do I mean? I have to admit that when I was younger and preaching door to door I thought that the Kingdom message was about how God was going to make the World we lived in into a Paradise, and that we could all enjoy life everlasting in this new world, with the hope of seeing dead loved ones resurrected. Why did I think that? That's what I was taught to preach, to warn people of the coming Armageddon and the promise of Paradise and the 1000 year messianic reign of Jesus Christ. I rarely ever preached the sole message of the Kingdom, we always preached about the *effects* of the Kingdom, how God would rid the world of wickedness and restore Earth to a Paradise, but rarely was the actual 'Kingdom' the sole message of our preaching work. I don't ever recall going house to house telling people the good news that Jehovah enthroned Jesus as King in 1914. Remember, this is their Kingdom message! That Jesus Christ became King and began his invisible presence or 2nd coming from the Heavens. Yet, I cannot ever recall myself or any JW I went into field ministry with preach this message. So it's actually fair to say that the Jehovah's Witnesses are not even faithful in preaching their own "gospel of the Kingdom".

When it comes down to it, most Witnesses don't even recognize that their "Kingdom message" actually revolves around the year 1914. Many of them view their message as one of Armageddon fast approaching or Paradise Earth, or the resurrection of dead loved ones. What is just as telling is what is usually lacking from their Kingdom message presentation. Ask any Witnesses whom you encounter, ask them what their "Good news" is and you'll likely get a variety of responses ranging from the Messianic Kingdom and Paradise Earth, but you will rarely hear a message that is based supremely on the Person of Jesus Christ. Yes, the Witness will occasionally throw in their Kingdom presentation at the door how the ransom sacrifice of Jesus opens the way for the opportunity to receive everlasting life, but they fail to realize the centrality of the Christian gospel is all about Jesus.

THE GOSPEL OF CHRIST

The Good News of Jesus Christ according to the Bible is not that Jesus became King of God's Kingdom in 1914, but that King Jesus died an atoning sacrifice for our sins, was buried and was rose again on the 3rd day. The Apostle Paul established what was the good news or gospel that has the power for salvation, he wrote:

"Now I make known to YOU, brothers, **the good news which I declared to YOU**, which YOU also received, in which YOU also stand, **through which YOU are also being saved**, with the speech with which I declared the good news to YOU, if YOU are holding it fast, unless, in fact, YOU became believers to no purpose. For I handed on to YOU, among **the first things**, that which I also received, **that Christ died for our sins** according to the Scriptures; and that **he was buried**, yes, that **he has been raised up the third day** according to the Scriptures".- 1 Corinthians 15:1-4 NWT

No mention of 1914, Paradise Earth, or Armageddon. The message of the good news is that the King has rescued and adopted a people unto himself through his death, and not only that but that King of that Kingdom lives! The Kingdom message is Jesus offered up for our sins and risen again to glory. The Jehovah's Witness needs to be shown that the good news is not about 1914, a religious organization, or even a Paradise; no the good news *is* Jesus Christ. Jesus is the good news, he is the fulfillment of God's Kingdom, the head of the Church, the prince and author of creation, and he is the "Yes" of God's promises. (2 Corinthians 1:20) God had a plan for redemption when Adam and Eve rebelled in the Garden, he had "good news" if you would. Yahweh had promised that a "seed" would come and strike the head of the serpent, doing away with the works and effects the serpent would have on mankind. (Genesis 3:15) Jesus is that seed; he is the "good news" to come, the very fulfillment of Messianic prophecy. Now the JW's agree that Genesis 3:15 is a Messianic reference to Christ Jesus, but they miss the implication and ultimately its fulfillment. God was giving humanity a glimpse into the Gospel of Salvation in that very first prophecy after the fall, and he was demonstrating that the whole story of redemption would come ultimately through his Son, the Messiah. The seed would be "bruised in the heel", indicating this promised one would experience death, but the seed would ultimately "crush" the head of the serpent, foreshadowing Christ's death and resurrection, the Good news! Why is Jesus' death, burial and resurrection such "good news" as opposed to the 1914 gospel message of Jehovah's Witnesses?

Jesus' death, burial and resurrection open the door of freedom and salvation. You see, the gospel of Jehovah's Witnesses is really no good news at all, for they say that they have the "hope" to live in a better world, the "hope" of a resurrection, a "hope" of eternal life. The reason I put quotation marks around the word hope in relation to JW's is because when the Witness says they have "hope" they mean that they have the opportunity to attain those things if they remain faithful to the Watchtower Society, and endure to the end. But the Bible refers to hope as something unfailing, without disappointment, and as complete assurance. Paul wrote "proven character produces hope. **This hope will not disappoint us,** because God's love has been poured out in our hearts through the Holy Spirit who was given to us." (Romans 5:4-5, HCSB) The good news of Jesus Christ produces true hope based upon God's love, it does not produce disappointment and disillusion as the so-called good news of the Watchtower.

But what does the good news mean to us? What exactly does it liberate us from? Hebrews 2:14-15 says "Now since the children have flesh and blood in common, Jesus also shared in these, so that **through His death** He might destroy the one holding the power of death—that is, the Devil— and **free those who were held in slavery** all their lives by the fear of death." The gospel frees us from the fear of Death; it destroys the grip of Satan over our lives, and leads us into a hope without disappointment. "This has now been made evident through the appearing of our Savior Christ Jesus, who has **abolished death** and has **brought life** and **immortality** to light **through the gospel.**" (2 Timothy 1:10. HCSB)

As a Jehovah's Witness I felt conflicted, I really believed in the message I preached, I really wanted to warn people of the coming destruction and also comfort them with the hope of a Paradise. But I felt as if I was offering them a product that they would likely not be able to afford. What do I mean? The Watchtower gospel says that if one lives righteously on their own merits, if *they* turn their lives around and follow everything taught by the Society, then maybe, just maybe if Jehovah finds them worthy, they will enter the new system. I was preaching a hope I wasn't even sure I had even attained. I was always told growing up that no one can ever say or know for sure that they are "saved" until after Armageddon. Does that really sound like good news? This is exactly what I was preaching to people, that if they start studying with Jehovah's Witnesses, going to Kingdom Hall meetings, preach from door to door, give talks at the meetings, cut their hair, not grow facial hair, and conform and become obedient to a multi-million dollar printing corporation that they might... if their obedient even till death or Armageddon, be awarded everlasting life in their utopia.

Therein lays the Gospel difference between the Good News of the Bible, and the illusion given by Jehovah's Witnesses, that through the death and resurrection of Jesus those who believe and trust in Jesus are saved, sealed, delivered, forgiven and accepted. Jesus did not die for "maybes", he died and rose again for your certainty, so that anyone who may "believe in the name of the Son of God... **may know that you have eternal life.**" (1 John 5:13) Because the good news is that Jesus is not dead but is alive he "is able also to **save completely** those who are approaching God through him, because he is always alive to plead for them." (Hebrews 7:25, NWT) Some translations say "he is able also to save them to the **uttermost**", what an incredible hope to share with Jehovah's Witnesses! As a Witness I was not aware that Jesus Christ could save me "completely" or to the uttermost, therefore I worked and strived to be as perfect as I could, knowing that the ransom sacrifice of Jesus only opened the way for the prospect of eternal life, but that he would only grant it to the worthy. The gospel of the Watchtower is not about salvation in Christ Jesus, it is built upon a rock-less foundation and the lie that Jesus has already returned in 1914. The differences in our gospels have many implications and doctrinal disputes, therefore in the next two chapters I want to go deeper into the topic of salvation in the Watchtower and in Christ, and also the manner of Christ resurrection and future return. But before then, I want to encourage you to give a Jehovah's Witness a witness of the true gospel of Jesus Christ.

SHARE THE GOOD NEWS!

I've noted multiple times throughout this book, sharing the gospel with Jehovah's Witnesses is not easy. But this good news is worth sharing, especially to those who are holding onto an empty gospel. Beyond the suit and tie, there is an unseen spiritual battle going on when the Witness comes knocking on your door, and we cannot afford as heralds of the gospel to not pick up our shield and sword and fight. (Ephesians 6:11-17) The weapons of our warfare are not earthly but spiritual, and the way we wage spiritual war is by declaring the truth over the lost and deceived, and Jehovah's Witnesses are no exception. Jude 3 says we must "contend for the faith" for it is something worth defending and fighting for. I am not advocating that we try and spend our morning refuting the Witness who comes knocking, for fruitless debating gets a Christian nowhere. Rather we should demonstrate the fruits of the Spirit which are love, joy, peace, patience, kindness, goodness, faith, gentleness, and self-control. (Galatians 5:22-23) Spiritual warfare is won not by retaliation or better debate performance, but by Christ in you. (1 John 4:4) That is why the Bible describes the spiritual state of Jehovah's Witnesses and the World in the following: "In their case, the god of this age has blinded the minds of the unbelievers so they **cannot see the light of the gospel** of the glory of Christ, who is the image of God." If you notice how the gospel message of Jehovah's Witnesses is centered on their organization it should not come as a surprise for true Christians "are not **proclaiming ourselves but Jesus Christ as Lord**, and ourselves as your slaves because of Jesus." (2 Corinthians 4:4-5, HCSB)

Be patient, as we understand that our message is spiritually discerned only by the work of the Holy Spirit and will be dismissed as foolishness by the Witnesses. (1 Corinthians 2:14) Love as you endeavor to share the good news of salvation in Jesus, for the love of Christ is what compels us to do so. (2 Corinthians 5:14) And have joy as you let your light shine before the JW who is in desperate need of the witness of the Risen King of God's Kingdom, even our Lord Jesus Christ. Point them to Jesus, the "Chief Agent and Perfecter of our faith" (Hebrews 12:2, NWT), and be "ambassadors for Christ, certain that God is appealing through us. We plead on Christ's behalf, "Be reconciled to God.'" (2 Corinthians 5:20, HCSB) The Gospel of Jesus is a gospel of reconciliation, so be an ambassador of peace, and be a witness of Jesus the Prince of Peace and his coming Kingdom. (Acts 1:8)

"Keep your attention on **Jesus Christ as risen from the dead** and descended from David. **This is according to my gospel.**" – 2 Timothy 2:8

CHAPTER 16

BORN AGAIN

"Truly, truly, I say to you, unless one is born again he cannot see the kingdom of God." (John 3:3, ESV) A Pharisee by the name of Nicodemus came to Jesus by night to compliment Jesus and praise him for the teachings and miracles he had performed. Nicodemus even went as so far to declare that Jesus was truly from God and that "God is with him"! How did Jesus respond to the flattery and praises from this ruler? He told him that he needed to be born again in order to see God's Kingdom. I often think about how a conversation between a Jehovah's Witness and Jesus would go. I imagine the Witness would begin offering up complimentary words of flattery to Jesus, praising his teachings and obedience to his Father, thanking him for the ransom sacrifice. I imagine Jesus without even a blink, pierce into their souls and cut through all the flattery and tell them, "You must be born again." Like Nicodemus, I see the Witness protesting and questioning Jesus as to "How can these things be?" (John 3:3-9) It had never occurred to Nicodemus that he needed anything other than his religion to save him, he believed that his standing as a Pharisee guaranteed him a chance to see God's kingdom. Jehovah's Witnesses likewise believe that association with their organization is all that is needed for a right standing before God. Yet Jesus didn't seem to be impressed with Nicodemus' religion or the organization of the Pharisees, instead Jesus understood his true need and addressed it. Nicodemus needed to be born again. Nicodemus was in need of salvation.

Likewise today, Jehovah's Witnesses are in need to salvation. In fact the Watchtower has convinced millions of Jehovah Witnesses that they have no need to be born again. Regarding the new birth the Society has written: "What, then, did Jesus mean when he stated that one must be born again to "enter into the kingdom of God"? He meant that one needs to be **born again in order to become a ruler with Christ in heaven**. Simply put, the purpose of the **new birth** is to prepare a **limited group** of humans for heavenly ruler- ship." –*The Watchtower*, April 1st, 2009

In essence the Watchtower Society has shut the door for the majority of Jehovah's Witnesses to ever be "born again", for they teach that only the 144,000 anointed Christians have the need to be born again since they are the only ones who will reign and be with Jesus. The Watchtower effectively shuts out the "great crowd" of Witnesses out of the Kingdoms gate, since it is taught that there are two classes or kinds of Christians; one that is the "great crowd" of "other sheep" who will live forever on Paradise Earth, then the "anointed" brothers and heirs of Christ, the 144,000 who alone are members of the "New Covenant". (Matthew 23:13) Witnesses do not believe that being "born again" and "saved" are synonymous since the Watchtower teaches that the new birth is associated with heavenly life which is reserved for the 144,000. However the distinction of two class Christians is simply not Biblical, for the Bible speaks of "one hope to which you were called", (Ephesians 4:4) and the hope of every Christian is to be with Christ. (Philippians 1:20-23; 3:20) As outlined in the chapter "<u>Death, Heaven & Paradise</u>", the Scriptures are clear in that all Christians will be with Jesus, and that the re-creation of the ages is the establishment of heavenly Jerusalem. God's Kingdom will be physically and forever established on the Earth, where the saints along with Yahweh God will reign and dwell with our Maker, as was the original design and intent in the Garden of Eden. Instead of focusing so much on the distinction of class in Watchtower theology, it is more important to get to the heart of the matter which is the salvation of our dear JW friends.

How can we demonstrate to JW's that being born again is essential to their eternity? The majority of Witnesses including myself saw no need to be "born again". In fact, I never wanted to be born again because I believed that salvation was dependent on my continued association with the organization, including my works and obedience to the organization. Jehovah's Witnesses do not believe that they themselves are saved. I have heard so many JW's say, "No one can say or know that they are saved!" And this is precisely what they must come to understand, that the reason they think no JW can say their saved is because they are not, because no practicing JW is born again in a New Testament sense. Many Witnesses will talk about "putting on the new personality", but they believe that this is a separate action than the new birth. I could testify that in our preaching work we knocked on doors offering an empty sale that they could have salvation if they do X Y and Z but yet we ourselves have not attained the prize we are offering. What kind of good news is that? According to Jesus, since JW's reject the new birth, they are in the flesh, which is the sinful nature. "What has been born from the **flesh is flesh**, and what has been **born from the spirit is spirit**. Do not marvel because I told you, YOU people **must be born again**." (John 3:6-7, NWT) Even though Jesus said not to marvel at this statement, the Witness stays marveled and puzzled because they refuse to obey their Master. Clearly Jesus is teaching that those who have been born into flesh, which is all of mankind, is walking in flesh which is to say walking in sin, for the psalmist said "With error I was brought forth with birth pains, and in **sin my mother conceived me**." (Psalm 51:5, NWT) The New Testament describes man's fallen condition in the following; "As for you, you were **dead** in your **transgressions** and **sins**". (Ephesians 2:1, NIV) The JW's do believe in original sin, that we have inherited this condition from our father Adam, yet they fail to realize the true intent of Jesus' words, that a carnal son or daughter of Adam must become born again in order to receive a different nature, one that is not of flesh but of spirit. The JW needs to be shown that if they have not received new natures, a new birth, then they are still walking in the flesh, and the Apostle Paul wrote that "Those who are in the realm of the **flesh cannot please God**." (Romans 8:8, NIV) Notice the contrast in the very next verse in relation to those who are born again and have been born of the Spirit, "You, however, are not in the realm of the flesh but are in the realm of **the Spirit**, if indeed the Spirit of God **lives in you**. And if anyone **does not** have the **Spirit of Christ**, they **do not belong to Christ**." (Romans 8:9, NIV) The Witness must see that the only Biblical distinction or classes there are, you are either in Christ or you're not, either you are born again or you are in the flesh, either you are saved or you are lost.

As believers we whom God has granted new birth have been shown the greatest mercy, and have been given the greatest gift. "In his great mercy he (God the Father) has given us **new birth into** a **living hope** through the resurrection of Jesus Christ from the dead, and into an **inheritance** that can never perish, spoil or fade—kept in heaven for you", and "For you have been **born again,** not of perishable seed, but of imperishable, through the living and enduring **word of God**... And this is the **word that was preached** to you." (1 Peter 1:3-4, 23-25, NIV) As in the previous chapter, we are called to be ambassadors of Christ, which means we are also ambassadors of a living hope through the new birth. As it is written, "Therefore, if anyone **is in Christ,** he is a **new creation;** the old has gone, the **new** has come!" (2 Corinthians 5:17, NIV) Being born again is an act of God; it is God giving you a new heart as prophesied in Ezekiel 36:26, "I will give you a **new heart** and put a **new spirit** in you; I will **remove** from you your **heart of stone** and give you a **heart of flesh**." (NIV) Pray and lead to JW to the Christ who said, "You *must* be born again!"

SALVATION BY WORKS OR BY FAITH?

The Jehovah's Witnesses believe that they are the only ones who will be collectively "saved" at Armageddon, however they teach that salvation is dependent on how you live in this present world, and if you measure up to Jehovah's standard. They also believe that they can be saved by identifying the Watchtower as God's organization, and serving God as a part of them. The Society has written, "**Only Jehovah's Witnesses,** those of the anointed remnant and the 'great crowd,' ... have **any Scriptural hope** of **surviving** the impending **end** of this doomed system." (*The Watchtower*, September 1st, 1989) The Society has even outlined a 4 step way to attain salvation, as outlined in the February 15, 1983, Watchtower magazine, the first requirement is "Taking in knowledge" of God, Christ and his purposes here on the Earth. The second requirement is to "obey God's laws", which laws? The ones the Watchtower picks and interprets for them. The third is that "we be associated with **God's channel, his organization**... To **receive everlasting life** in the earthly Paradise **we must** identify that **organization** and serve God as part of it." And finally, the fourth requirement is to be loyal to God, his Kingdom and his organization by preaching to others. "God requires that prospective subjects of his Kingdom support his government by **loyally advocating** his Kingdom rule to others". A few things were mentioned in that Watchtower article regarding salvation, but something incredibly important was seemingly left out. Any guesses? Left out was

Jesus' death, burial and resurrection and the ransom that was paid through his blood. Why would the Watchtower leave that out? Because they believe that one has to constantly "do" in order to please and impress God.

When I was a Jehovah's Witnesses I often found myself and those around me in constant stages of depression, as I never felt good enough, for I was constantly attending meetings, going street witnessing and door to door, studying the Watchtower magazine and commenting during the meetings. It was a never ending list of chores to do, and I never knew when and what would be enough to satisfy Jehovah. When I was younger I was constantly compared and judged by others, I once had an elder in my congregation ask me why I wasn't commenting as much as the other kids during the meetings. Even as a child I would become frustrated and sad, I wanted to be accepted by my God and my religious community. Although many Witnesses and including some quotes in Watchtower publications pay lip service to Jesus and the ransom sacrifice, but what they really mean is that the atonement of Jesus merely gives us the opportunity for salvation, it doesn't actually guarantee it. Some JW's will even say and profess that salvation is a free gift and that they cannot attain it by works. Yet this is merely a JW's attempt to sound Biblical, for in practice it is the exact opposite. Works is not only required, it is demanded, and the elders in the congregation regularly check to see if the members of the Hall are working enough in the preaching ministry. At the end of every month JW's are required to report how many hours they preached during that month, how many Bible studies they conducted, and how many pieces of literature did they distribute. The Society claims that this is solely for the purpose of keeping track of the Worldwide work being conducted by JW's, but in practice it is used to measure the spiritual state of every JW in the Kingdom Hall. Every JW and those studying with JW's know well in their hearts that if they do not do enough works, they may be destroyed by God at Armageddon. Witnesses who are not as active in the congregation are looked down upon as "spiritually weak" or "spiritually unstable".

One of the reasons why I began to doubt my faith was, to be honest, I was tired. I came to a realization that my whole life in this organization I will have to strive to be as righteous as I possibly could be, to preach as much as I could, to try and perfect my fallen flesh. I knew that enough would never be enough to satisfy the Holy God of the Bible. Yet in Jesus not only did I find salvation, I also found assurance and rest. The Bible paints salvation in a very different light then how the Watchtower Society portrays it. While the Watchtower Society stresses works and obedience to an organization, the Bible teaches salvation as a free gift from God, through faith in Jesus Christ. Ephesians 2:8-9 says "For it is by **grace** you have **been saved**, through **faith**—and this is not from **yourselves**, it is the **gift of God**— **not by works**, so that no one can boast." (NIV) No amount of works can ever grant you salvation, but it can only be received by God's free grace, his undeserved kindness, so that at the end God can receive all the glory, and man will have no reason to boast in himself, rather he can boast in the Lord. (1 Corinthians 1:30-31) The immediate apologetic verse by the JW will be James 2:24-26, which states that "faith without works is dead". When I was a JW I would argue that in order for anyone to be justified, they needed to prove themselves worthy by works so as to prove their faith is genuine. How Ephesians 2:8 and James 2:24 be harmonized? The major difference between Jehovah's Witnesses and Christianity at this point is that the Witnesses believe that the works are the **root** or the cause of salvation, and the Christian believes that works are the **fruitage** of the salvation they already have. The JW works to be saved, and the Christian works because he already *is* saved! You must show the Witness that salvation cannot be attained by works, for is salvation is by grace then it can no longer be by works for as the Apostle Paul wrote, "Now if it is **by undeserved kindness** (grace), it is no longer **due to works**; otherwise, the undeserved kindness **no longer proves** to be **undeserved kindness**." (Romans 11:6, NWT) In Titus 3:5-6 we find that salvation is "owing to **no works in righteousness** that we had performed, but according to his **mercy he saved** us through the bath that brought us to life and through the **making of us new by holy spirit**. This [spirit] he poured out richly upon us through Jesus Christ our Savior, that, after being **declared righteous** by virtue of the **undeserved kindness** of that one, we might become heirs according to a hope of everlasting life." (NWT) Notice who is doing the saving and how; "according to *his* mercy *he* saved us", and he is "making us new by the Holy Spirit", and we are "declared righteous by virtue" of *his* underserved kindness. No mention of joining and following an organization as a requirement for salvation, rather the only requirement seen is to "Believe on the Lord Jesus and you *will* be saved". (Acts 16:30-31)

Jehovah Witnesses will try and argue that if all it takes to be saved is to "believe" then that means that you can just say you believe and yet live like the world and be in sin. However we must explain to them that our salvation and freedom in Christ is not license to sin, for Paul dealt with this very claim in Romans 6:1-4, "What should we say then? Should we continue in sin so that grace may multiply? Absolutely not! How can we who died to sin still live in it? Or are you unaware that all of us who were baptized into Christ Jesus were baptized into His death? Therefore we were buried with Him by baptism into death, in order that, just as Christ was raised from the dead by the glory of the Father so we too may walk in a new way of life." (HCSB) Being born again means taking on a new spiritual nature, the Christian being saved by grace through faith in Jesus *will* be conformed to God's Word, walk in repentance and faith, and ultimately be kept by the power of God. Salvation is not based upon works committed in righteousness, for even Jehovah describes "all our righteous acts are like filthy rags" before him. (Isaiah 64:6, NIV) "But God demonstrates his own love for us in this: While we were **still sinners, Christ died for us...** Not only is this so, but we also boast in God through our Lord Jesus Christ, through whom we have **now received reconciliation.**" (Romans 5:8-11, NIV)

IN CHRIST ALONE

Jesus is enough, Jesus is Sufficient! Unfortunately the Watchtower Society has tried to hide the sufficiency of Christ by adding unbiblical requirements and burdens upon the shoulders of Jehovah's Witnesses. I believe that many Witnesses deep down inside feel the burden and incredible weight of the pressures of trying to measure up to the Watchtowers standards, I have personally seen fellow Witnesses go to the brink of insanity trying to measure up or dealing with the guilt of not measuring up. For instance many ex-JW's who get disfellowshiped often time fall into a deep depression and consider suicide. The pressures and anguish of being separated from your loved ones and being excluded from fellowship with your own family members takes an incredible emotional and psychological toll. Maybe, just maybe the well-groomed Witness who just knocked on your door is battling short-comings and depression. How vital it is that we offer them a hope based upon the truth and reality of the Gospel of Jesus! JW's need to hear about the true love of God and that God's love is not conditional but unconditional.

JW's believe that one can lose their standing or salvation with God by committing any sin or wrongdoing, but Jesus said "My sheep **listen** to my voice, and I know them, and they **follow** me. And I give them everlasting life, and they will by **no means ever be destroyed,** and **no one will snatch them out of my hand.**" (John 10:27-28, NWT) Jesus tells us that none of his sheep will ever be destroyed or snatched from his hands, true believers lay secure in the hands of the Savior. "Who will **separate** us from the love of the Christ? ... To the contrary, in all these things we are coming off **completely victorious** through him that loved us. For I am convinced that neither **death** nor **life** nor **angels** nor **governments** nor **things now** here nor **things to come** nor **powers** nor **height** nor **depth** nor **any other creation** will be able to **separate** us from **God's love** that is **in Christ Jesus our Lord.**" (Romans 8:35-39, NWT) Nothing in all of creation can separate a child of God from his Heavenly Father. This is a love and an assurance that the JW has been looking for their entire life, and they will not find it in the Watchtower, but only in Christ. Christians "are being **safeguarded by God's power** through faith for a salvation ready to be revealed in the last period of time." (1 Peter 1:5, NWT) The Jehovah's Witnesses believe that they must endure to the end to be saved; Christians know we will endure to the end, because our salvation depends not on us, but on He who saves. When the JW hears a Christian speaking of the salvation and security they have in Christ, they may be scuffle at first, but once you begin to give Biblical reasons as to your salvation and security, deep down inside the Witness might just be intrigued. The first time I began to read certain Bible verses on salvation and security in Christ, I thought to myself, "This is too simple, too easy... It can't be!" JW's have been conditioned to view salvation as something almost unattainable. Yet by prayerfully witnessing and sharing this Bible hope, the life of a JW can be changed forever.

We can also demonstrate to them that they can *know* that they can have eternal life! As I mentioned before, growing up the JW religion it was always taught and preached that no one can claim salvation in this life since we were all imperfect and needed to work for our salvation and endure to the end. Believing in Jesus, however, means that we can know for a certainty that our sins have been forgiven and that we have eternal life. 1 John 5:12 in the NWT reads: "I write YOU these things that **YOU may know** that YOU have life everlasting, YOU who put YOUR faith in the **name of the Son of God.**" With Jesus there is no "maybes" for all the promises of God are Yes in him! (2 Corinthians 1:20) Jesus also said that "He that hears my word and believes him that sent me **has everlasting life**, and he does not come into judgment but has passed over from **death to life.**"(John 5:24, NWT) The Jehovah's Witness live in a constant fear of judgment; they feel that if they slip up right before Armageddon that they may lose all their hope of being saved, yet the Bible says that those who live in fear have not experienced

God's love. "There is **no fear in love**, but **perfect love throws fear outside**, because fear exercises a restraint. Indeed, he that is **under fear has not** been made **perfect in love**." (1 John 4:18, NWT) The new birth means that we are included in the covenant and promises of God, no longer having to be in constant fear of judgment, rather we can "approach the throne of grace with boldness", knowing that Jesus our High Priest and mediator has paid the price for our redemption in full. (Hebrews 4:16, HCSB)

Ultimately, being born again unto a newness of life and salvation is all by the name and power of Jesus. My view of Jesus as a JW was a weak one, for I believed that Jesus could not truly save, that my salvation depended just as much on me as it did Christ. Yet in the Scriptures I found a Jesus that had the power "to **save completely** those who are approaching God through him". (Hebrews 7:25, NWT) As a Christian I now trust fully in the saving work of Jesus Christ, and that by receiving a new nature by new birth I now have the Holy Spirit dwelling in me who is the "deposit **guaranteeing our inheritance** until the redemption of those who are God's possession", (Ephesians 1:13-14, NIV) and through the power of the Spirit living in me I will be kept until the end and will run the race of life with full endurance as I look to Jesus. (Hebrews 12:1-2) Jesus is sufficient, Jesus is enough- To Him be the Glory, the author of our salvation, both now and forevermore! "Furthermore, there is **no salvation in anyone else**, for there is not another name under heaven that has been given among men **by which we must get saved**."- Acts 4:12, NWT

CHAPTER 17

MY WITNESS

In this book you have hopefully learned about the teachings and beliefs of Jehovah's Witness. I also hope that in the process you have come to understand Jehovah's Witnesses as people, not just as a religious sect. The reason I have decided to leave this testimony till the very end is because I believe once you attain knowledge about a specific group of people like Jehovah's Witnesses, it is important that you understand the story of a specific person who grew up in it and lived it. My story is the story of every Jehovah's Witness who finds freedom and forgiveness in Christ. This is our story, our pain, our burdens, our tears, our sacrifices, our cross and our victory. My story may be unique, as is everybody else's, for everyone's story although different, is also all the same. My testimony is simple; I was once lost, but now I am found. I was once blind, but now I see.

Sharing my life through the pages of this book is not easy, I am well aware of the resent and disappointment of my family members who know of my writing this book. It is not my intention to distance the ones I love, because I am not the one distancing myself, and I believe that this is a book worth writing. Retelling my story reopens wounds once thought healed, and reminds me of the constant divide between me and the ones I love. I absolutely love Jehovah's Witnesses with all my heart, for as I have written from the start of this book, Jehovah's Witnesses are my family; My mother, my father, my brother, my sister, my nieces and nephew, my aunts and uncles and my cousins. Of two generations of Jehovah's Witnesses, I am the only one who has left the organization to serve and follow Jesus Christ. This has not been an easy road for me; I have been ridiculed, kicked out of my home, homeless, abandoned, forsaken and deserted by the ones I love. I have many friends and family members who have not even as much even looked at me. I've been mocked and have been the target of malicious rumors and stories throughout my family and former congregation of Jehovah's Witnesses. But it wasn't always so.

I grew up in a very devout and loving second-generation, Hispanic Jehovah's Witness family in Hartford, CT. From an early age, my life revolved around 'Jehovah's organization'. My mother made the practice of being an auxiliary and regular pioneer, someone who devoted at that time more than 70 hours of preaching a month, and I would regularly go preaching door to door with her, knocking on people's doors and telling them about Jehovah. I loved telling people about God and Bible stories such as the flood of Noah and mighty Samson, even in Kindergarten I would draw pictures of Bible scenes and tell my classmates and teachers about my faith in God's Word. I considered myself a pretty typical child, I loved playing video games, spending time outdoors, and getting into trouble ever so often. The only difference between me and other children was that they were able to participate in birthday and holiday celebrations. I know for a lot of people who grow up in and left the Witnesses, not being able to participate in celebrations was very traumatic in their upbringing, but for me it was something that I embraced. Being a Jehovah's Witness made me standout, it made me distinct from everyone else and I enjoyed it. When other kids would see me not participating in a birthday, Halloween or Valentine's Day celebration they would ask me why, and I gladly told them it was because I was one of Jehovah's Witnesses and I believed that those celebrations were wrong. Many teachers and students were intrigued and perplexed by my zeal and beliefs.

Since too much outside interaction was discouraged, as a family we would regularly engage with other JW families, being Hispanic and growing up in a Spanish Congregation, celebrations and get-togethers were often and exciting! I always looked forward to spending time with friends from the Kingdom Hall. Growing up in a bilingual home was challenging as a Jehovah's Witness since we attended Spanish services and my Spanish wasn't as good or polished as the other kids around me. I grew timid and intimidated when I began seeing other kids giving parts at the Kingdom Hall, such as reading Bible verses at the Theocratic Ministry School or giving comments in Spanish at the Watchtower Study. After a while I decided that I would not allow language from keeping me from serving my God. So finally at the age of 13, I felt that I was "ready" to commit my life to Jehovah God through water baptism. I was fully convinced that this religion was the only true faith, for the majority of my life I believed that I was in "the truth". I dedicated myself to this cause, this idea; I dedicated my life to an organization of men who claimed to be the only way to God.

TROUBLE IN PARADISE

I was always a curious boy, I loved asking "why?" to just about everything. From a fairly early age I began to see the need to better understand the reasons for my faith. As a teenager I started stumbling across a lot of material that would have been considered either apostate or anti-JW. I was shocked, how could anyone hate and write things against God's organization? I set out to debunk them and defend "the truth", because I believed with all my heart that if what I had was indeed the truth, then I had nothing to fear. I began defending "the truth" on the internet, debating Christians and anyone who would bring a charge against my beloved organization. I became known as a 'Watchtower apologist', and I was good. You see, intellectually I felt justified in nearly all my defenses of the organization. That has always been important to me, being intellectually satisfied and consistent. Despite what many in my family believe, it was not this interaction and debating that "confused" me and brainwashed me into leaving "the truth", in fact, doing all of that strengthened my faith. The first signs of trouble I had in God's "spiritual paradise", as JW's call their organization, was the inconsistency of the love they claim to have in their midst. By my early teenage years I was a young man in desperate need. My mother had been disfellowshipped, my parents were divorced, and I had been homeless with my mother more than once, taking care of her since she became very mentally instable after her disfellowshipping. Here I was, barely old enough to take care of myself, holding the remnants of my family upon my shoulders. How did the loving brothers care for us during that turbulent time? Well since my mother was disfellowshipped, we barely got even so much as a hand on our shoulders. I understood though, I justified it and shifted the blame to us, because the brothers were just being "faithful to Jehovah". But surely, they would help me, a baptized member of "the truth". What I discovered rather quickly, was that I was on my own. I had very little Witnesses my age who wanted to associate with me, very little elders or adults in the congregation who wanted to mentor or disciple me. I desperately yearned for the attention of my fellow brothers and sister, even switching to a new congregation in search of that love and companionship. I never found it. My mother eventually came back to "the truth" and was reinstated. But the loneliness never went away, I stood in the middle of an organization that brags to the outside world that there is so much love among their association of believers, yet I couldn't help but feel the breath of a cold, mechanical organization.

As a young man, I began to seek ways to fill that void by pursuing relationships with people who would meet and fill my need of companionship. Naturally, as young men and women do, I began to fall in love and become involved with romantic relationships. Throughout my time as a Witness being romantically involved with a non-Witness girl and then a baptized Witness, I had never committed any sins worthy of disfellowshipping. Although I felt in many ways deserted by my own people, I was nonetheless very faithful to the God and organization that I believed in. However, as time went by and as much as I tried to maintain active in the congregation and be social with other Witnesses, the more I felt alone. The perfect storm clouds of my life were gathering, I felt alone and abandoned by my faith and I began for the first time in my life to feel tired. I was tired. I remember asking myself, "How much more do I have to do to gain my peoples and my God's approval?" I had committed my life to this organization, put thousands of hours into advancing their message and knocking on doors. I felt like I was a dog chasing his tail and I was so sick of feeling ashamed and unworthy. What did I do with all my disappointments? I did what many other Witnesses do; I hid it under a mask of self-righteousness. I continued doing more and more works to seem outwardly righteous, making it seem as if all was good in Jehovah's "spiritual paradise". But something extraordinary happened, for the first time in my whole life as one of Jehovah's Witnesses, I received a witness.

LOVE, FORGIVENESS AND REDEMPTION

In a time desperation and loneliness, I reached out to a "born again" Christian who I would regularly debate with through YouTube. Originally I reached out because I was interested in debating and trying to convert him, but somewhere in that process, we developed an intimate friendship, something that I was craving from my own brothers at the Kingdom Hall. It turned from having weekly debates to just me pouring my heart to this man and he would listen and pray for me. In my mind, he had never won any of our debates, I was convinced that he was wrong, but he sincerely loved me in a Christ-like manner and never forced his views on me. In fact, I got to see humility, patience, friendship, and sincerity at work through this man. When he talked about his relationship with Jesus, and how Jesus delivered him for loneliness, guilt and shame. I envied him. I wanted what he had with Jesus, but I was unwilling to accept Christian beliefs. But for the first time ever, I received a witness from someone who followed Jesus Christ. Through that one sincere believer giving me a witness, the Lord began working on my heart. I slowly started seeing that my arguments in defense of the Watchtower were riddled with wholes. I began seeking after Jehovah in the Scriptures, and the more I turned to the Bible, the more I began to see the differences between the Watchtower magazine on my left hand and the Bible in my right hand. After tirelessly striving for approval and ultimately for salvation as a Jehovah's Witness, I began to see that there are not enough works in the universe that I could do to achieve everlasting life, for the Bible says, "By this **undeserved kindness**, indeed, YOU have been **saved through faith**; and this **not owing to YOU, it is God's gift**." (Ephesians 2:8, NWT) In my study of God's Word, I became stunned by the concept of grace or "underserved kindness" as the New World translates it. I was taught my whole life that if I didn't measure up to God's standards, I would be destroyed and crushed by Jehovah. The good news I was missing was that only one man has ever measured up to God's standard and that was Jesus Christ, and he was the one who was actually "crushed" by Jehovah in order to make satisfaction on my behalf! Grace offered me unconditional love, forgiveness and redemption, and at that point thought to myself that I could either continue to seem outwardly righteous, and rely on myself and an organization for salvation, or I could trust in Jesus. My only problem, I could not accept or believe that Jesus was God.

For months I began systematically on my own research what the Bible taught about salvation and the person and work of Jesus Christ. During my studies I became convinced that unless I became "born again", that I would be spiritually dead and still in the flesh. (John 3:3-7) I accepted that salvation was purely a gift of God, and that I was in need of that gift. But I still believed in many teachings of the Witnesses, but things were quickly unraveling. I can remember setting up a meeting with a few elders from my Hall and asked them if they could help me in understanding some of the things I was coming across in my study of the Bible. After speaking my heart to these elders, they asked me if I had looked up Watchtower publications for answers. I responded by saying that I was aware of the Society's official stance on the issues, and that I was not satisfied with the answers therein, thus why I was approaching them for guidance. The two elders who were meeting with me looked at each other and said "Well all we can do is direct you back to the Society's publications". With that statement, I left that meeting fully convinced that I was a sinner in need of God and not in need of man. I knew that I needed to be born again. I decided that I would not walk back into a Kingdom Hall until God revealed to me the plain truth of who Jesus Christ truly was. I came upon a breaking point, a crossroads. After months of searching God, seeking His Word and comparing it to what I had taught and defended, I sat down one afternoon and told God that I would not put down my Bible until he had given me an answer.

Many hours later, I began to feel frustrated and put my Bible down and looked up to Heaven and demanded Jehovah for an answer, I would not go to sleep unless I had the peace and answer that I wanted. All of sudden God opened my mind to the Scriptures and I could feel God connecting the thoughts and opening my mind to who Christ Jesus truly is. I rushed back to my Bible and I read Acts 7:54-60 in my New World Translation, where Stephen is facing death and raises his eyes to Heaven which reads: "And they went on casting stones at Stephen as he made appeal and said: "Lord Jesus, receive my spirit." In the footnote of my NWT Study edition on verse 59 in regard to the word "appeal" it said "Or, "invocation; prayer." In an instant it all made sense, I put my Bible down and raised my hands to Heaven and appealed and prayed to Jesus Christ for the first time in my life. I said "Lord Jesus, I do not know how you are what you are, but I know that you are God Almighty. Forgive me of following a false organization and forgive me of my sins, I surrender and worship you. Thank you Lord Jesus!" In that moment I had received the greatest witness of all, the witness of Jesus Christ himself.

That very moment I knew that I had been born again, dead to sin and alive to God in Christ. I immediately felt the love, forgiveness and redemption of Jesus Christ; it was like coming home, all of my guilt and shame was gone, I had become a new creation in Christ. Jesus said that "the one who comes to me **I will never cast out**", (John 6:37) and the Apostle Paul wrote, "Therefore, if anyone **is in Christ**, he is a **new creation**; old things have passed away, and look, new things have come." (2 Corinthians 5:17, HCSB)

The Lord immediately told me what I knew needed to be done, and He let me know that the road ahead was not going to be an easy one, but I heard in my heart the words "I will never leave you nor forsake you". Waking up the next morning was an incredible confirmation of what had happened the night before, for the first time I felt alive, the grass was literally greener and I saw beauty and purpose in everything that I saw. My new journey as a Christian was not an easy one, for I knew very little Christians and almost none in person. I had never stepped into a Christian Church, had no contact information with believers in my area, but I was never alone. I stopped attending the Kingdom Hall, which raised the suspicion of my family, and the Lord guided me to a Christian Church that took me in with open arms. I had to keep my new found faith a secret, for at the time I was living with my father at an aunt's house, and if they found out I would be kicked out immediately. Eventually my aunt discovered that I had attended a Church service and told my father. They called the elders and they set up a meeting to interrogate me. I was nervous, but never fearful for I knew the day would come and was prepared. I met with the body of elders with my father in the room, and I before a word could be exchanged I handed them my letter of disassociation, informing them that I no longer wished to be known as one of Jehovah's Witnesses and that I had repented of my sins and put my faith in Jesus, our Great God and Savior. (Titus 2:13) I saw my father next to me for the first time in my life break down and sob. Seeing that broke my heart, and what broke it even more was the cold faces of the elders as they look on with no words of comfort or hope. I left that meeting and later that night I was kicked out of my home with no place to go. This was the hardest time of my life, my family and friends viewed me as a traitor, I was homeless in the middle of the winter, yet I never remember a time in my life where I was most at peace. I was living in the reality of God's Word when it says "When my father and my mother forsake me, Then Jehovah will take me up." (Psalm 27:10, ASV) My new family in Christ quickly helped me meet my needs, and my loving mother came to my side and took me in.

I do not blame or hate my family and friends for the way they acted towards me, I understand them completely. I do not hate the Watchtower Bible and Tract Society, I pray for them. The next few years of my life was marred by pain, hardships, opposition and persecution even to this day because of my decision to follow Christ. But in the end I have found it to be more than worth it, for although I lost my entire world, I gained Christ. I have been far from perfect as a Christian; I have sinned and made many mistakes throughout my walk with Christ, but I walk with the assurance that He will pick me up from my sin and restore me to our God and Father. God has blessed me with so many opportunities to preach his Gospel and to help change the World and He has also since blessed me with a wonderful family in Christ, and a beautiful family at home. I am now a husband, a father, a friend, a son, a brother, and most importantly a follower of Jesus Christ. I hope that this book becomes a bridge, that by God's grace those within my family would read it and at least come to understand why I did what I did. Many in my family believe I am an apostate, but I want them to see that I am not an apostate, I am a Christian.

I AM A CHRISTIAN, NOT AN APOSTATE

Today, because of my convictions and decision to follow Christ Jesus instead of men, the Watchtower Society has bestowed upon me the title of "Apostate". The word Apostate literally means to "defect" from a religious or political view. To the Jehovah's Witnesses however, the word apostate means someone who is under the control and bidding of Satan the Devil. "**Satan** was the first creature to turn **apostate**. **Modern-day apostates** display **characteristics similar** to those of **the Devil**. Their mind may be poisoned by a critical attitude… They are not interested in learning about Jehovah or in serving him. **Like their father, Satan, apostates** target people of integrity." (*The Watchtower*, April. 15th, 2009)

I want my family and all Jehovah's Witnesses to know that I am not some boogeyman out to destroy their faith. I am not bent on bringing down the Watchtower or snatching away disciples after myself. I am nothing by myself, if I can accomplish one thing in regard to Jehovah's Witnesses, it is to love them and tell them about the only truth that sets man free, Jesus Christ, and making disciples for Him. Despite the label of "apostate", I am very interested in serving, knowing and exalting Jehovah God, because I am a Christian, not an "apostate".

I recently heard a discourse that was given at a district convention of Jehovah's Witnesses entitled "Truth brings, not Peace, but a Sword" which will be heard by millions of Jehovah's Witnesses at this years "God's Word is Truth!" district convention. The talk I heard was given by a Bethelite (a person who has served in a Watchtower facility) and lasted about 20 minutes. The talk was based upon Jesus' words in Matthew 10:34-36 which reads "Do not think I came to put peace upon the earth; I came to put, not peace, but a sword. For I came to cause division, with a man against his father, and a daughter against her mother, and a young wife against her mother-in-law. Indeed, a man's enemies will be persons of his own household." (NWT)

In this talk I heard the speaker talk about the importance of serving God and Christ and that we ought to be loyal to them, things that I totally affirm and believe. I then began to hear the speaker talk about how following Christ sometimes brings division in some families, something that I also believe in and have experienced. However the speaker goes even further when he explains that it isn't "the truth"(aka the Watchtower religion) that causes division, rather "that division is because of that family member who refuses to have union with Jehovah God and Jesus Christ and he opposes us." I came to a crossing point between what I read in the pages of the Watchtower and what I found in the Bible. I disassociated myself for finding faith in the person and work of Jesus Christ, I was not disfellowshipped. This statement from the convention talk troubles me and we see it time and time again in print through the pages of the Watchtower; I have never refused to be in fellowship or union with Jehovah and Jesus, in fact it was for that very reason that I left. Because I left the JW organization to follow Jesus Christ, in the eyes of the Watchtower and my JW relatives, I am an apostate. The tone of the organization when it comes to those who leave is a predictable us vs. them, we are right, anyone who leaves is wrong. How reassuring. For instance, the talk given at the 2013 JW Convention the speaker goes on to stress that if a member of that family leaves the organization, they automatically become "wrongdoers" who are the ones who "changed their relationship with Jehovah" and with JW family members. They shift the blame on the person who left; because of course there is never a legitimate reason to leave that religious organization. The speaker merely tells those who may have ex-JW family members to "respect Jehovah's arrangement for discipline." He also warned that "disloyalty to that arrangement results in more distress". In horrid fashion, the speaker likens disfellowshipped family members to "drug addicts or an alcoholic". Really?

This is what worries me, my family member who are still devout Jehovah's Witnesses who will be attending this year's convention and who will hear this very 20 minute talk, will in effect view me as an enemy, an apostate. It has been more than 5 years since I disassociated myself and was born again as a follower of Jesus (John 3:3-7), in those 5 years I have put a lot of effort to reconcile certain family relationships. In 5 years I went from being an outcast in my own family being disowned, to being respected by at least some of my dear family. I worry that in 20 minutes, 5 years of prayers, tears, and patience, will be undone. In 20 minutes I will likely become an enemy instead of a son, a brother, a cousin, and family. In 20 minutes I become the kin to a drug addict or alcoholic, instead of being recognized as a faithful husband, father and Christian.

In hypocritical fashion, the Watchtower Society published the article "Is it Wrong to Change Your Religion?" the July 2009 Awake says: "**No one should be forced** to worship in a way that he **finds unacceptable** or be made to **choose** between **his beliefs and his family**." This is a clear double standard, for they obviously make people choose between their religious conscious and their family. Ever since I was a little boy all I ever desired was to worship and serve the One True God, and when I began to understand that "the truth" was not simply a religious organization that was started in the late 1800's, but that "the truth" was in fact a Person, I was convinced that I had found the way. Why? Because when Jesus said, "I am the Way, the Truth and the Life", I believe he meant it. (John 14:6)

Jesus said "Whoever loves father or mother more than me is not worthy of me, and whoever loves son or daughter more than me is not worthy of me. And whoever does not take his cross and follow me is not worthy of me. Whoever **finds his life will lose it,** and whoever **loses his life for my sake will find it**."(Matthew 10:37-39) I have indeed lost all things for the sake of Christ, like Paul "I consider everything **a loss** because of the **surpassing worth of knowing Christ Jesus my Lord,** for whose sake I have lost all things."(Philippians 3:8) I want my family and every other Jehovah's Witness to understand that leaving their religion for Jesus doesn't make me an apostate, it makes me a Christian.

I never left Jehovah, I found Jehovah; well actually Jehovah found me. If Jehovah can find, save and transform me into a witness of Jesus, I am full of hope that He can do it with many more, including members of my own family. Beloved Christians, be the witness that Jesus called you to be. It is my prayer that you use this book to help JW's everywhere and be a witness so that you could open the eyes of those who are being misled by the Watchtower, so that Jehovah's Witnesses everywhere may see the light of the glory of the gospel of Christ. (2 Corinthians 4:4) Amen.

25200959R00090

Made in the USA
Charleston, SC
18 December 2013